Praise for *The Succe*

The Success Trap fearlessly shines light into all the nooks and crannies of this complex issue, including the personal, professional, cultural and environmental dynamics in the workplace. For 25 years I have coached professionals in breaking free of the personal limitations that kept them stuck, fearful and feeling powerless. *The Success Trap* is a guide that provides practical tools and hope for healthier organizational environments and empowered leaders to live more true to their personal values and wellbeing. FRAN FISHER, MASTER CERTIFIED COACH, AND AUTHOR, *CALLING FORTH GREATNESS: SEVEN COACHING WISDOMS FOR TRANSFORMING YOUR LIFE*

Long-term achievement means finding long-term behaviours that will deliver success. Amina Aitsi-Selmi's considered thoughts start with science to embrace her extensive coaching experience. If you want to change your life, you need to change yourself, and this book will show you how. PROFESSOR MICHAEL MAINELLI, ALDERMAN AND SHERIFF OF THE CITY OF LONDON

Even for those not blessed with a grounding dose of self-doubt, the career success that seems for a while only to breed success can suddenly also bring burnout, a loss of the creative urge or a reluctance to strike out in new directions. By helping you through this high-achiever paradox, Amina Aitsi-Selmi can show you how to rekindle that sense of true purpose that gets the best out of you and all those who work around you. EDWINA MORETON OBE, FORMER DIPLOMATIC EDITOR, *THE ECONOMIST*

This is a timely and much needed book, especially now that the old world of work is being recalibrated and new ways of working are emerging. Toxic workplaces will not be able to survive and many people will want to break free to work at humane workplaces or work for themselves. I warmly welcome this book. PROFESSOR VLATKA HLUPIC, AUTHOR, *THE MANAGEMENT SHIFT* AND *HUMANE CAPITAL*

What most people know about Dr Amina Aitsi-Selmi is that she is a trusted adviser on leadership and careers to highly successful doctors and high achievers. She's a world-class expert at guiding the most successful people on the planet out of jobs and careers that have trapped them, into lives that fulfil them. She has a track record in helping clients do exceptional things.

What most people don't know about Amina is that she is one of the most extraordinary and courageous people you could ever meet. She is also one of the most humble people I know, which is why – before I tell you why this book is life-changing – I need to tell you about Amina.

She left Algeria due to the civil war, as a young child, eventually studying medicine at Cambridge University. She has a Master's degree from the London School of Hygiene and Tropical Medicine and a PhD in Epidemiology and Statistics from University College London. She's a Clinician Scientist and a UN adviser. She has been a Consultant in International Public Health – with a focus on evidence-informed disaster risk reduction. And a Consultant in Global Health Security at the Royal Institute of International Affairs, Chatham House. She's been an Honorary Senior Clinical Lecturer at the Institute of Global Health. And she volunteered with Médecins Sans Frontières in South Sudan – one of the world's most dangerous countries.

The Success Trap will take you through the mindset shifts and strategic steps needed to create what you truly want in your life. If you're a top performer, this is a must-read. RICH LITVIN, FOUNDER, 4PC – A COMMUNITY OF THE WORLD'S LEADING COACHES

Amina Aitsi-Selmi has written a timely, deep and practical book. The illusion of stability and predictability is disappearing fast. We will all make many career choices in our lives. She explains how to make those choices by uncovering your individual answers to four fundamental questions: *who are you, what do you value, what do you want and what do you love?* Answering these questions, and breaking habits of thought and behaviour, creates freedom and awareness. You travel beyond fear of change or goal addiction to work that is fulfilling and meaningful, and Amina is your wise guide. DR STEPHEN BURT, LEADERSHIP COACH, AND AUTHOR, *THE ART OF LISTENING IN COACHING AND MENTORING*

The Success Trap is a superb guide on how to overcome fear and embrace the entrepreneurial spirit within all of us. The principles in this book enable you to navigate career choices, discover passions and make the impossible possible. Learn to overcome the self-doubt plaguing your mind and listen to the maddening little voice in your head that says, 'What's really stopping me? Why wait for others to capitalize on my idea?' Only then can you begin your first steps towards making your dreams come true. MICHAEL ZHOU, CEO, LIVING SKY TECHNOLOGIES, AND CO-FOUNDER, ALIBABA

Success and happiness are not the same thing. Yet despite this, many people stay in superficially successful but deeply unfulfilling jobs that they don't like. Aitsi-Selmi addresses this paradox, writing with compassion and insight into the modern world of work. Everyone who has ever worried about whether they are happy at work will find something valuable in this book, which provides an eminently practical approach to escaping the Success Trap and living a happier and more fulfilled life. PROFESSOR GERAINT REES FMEDSCI, UCL PRO-VICE-PROVOST (AI), AND DEAN, UCL FACULTY OF LIFE SCIENCES

As a society and as individuals we should want more from our working lives. Amina Aitsi-Selmi's insights, gathered from many years of coaching, help us understand why we accept less than we should and how we might go about making our work an integral part of living the best life we can. MATTHEW TAYLOR, CHIEF EXECUTIVE, THE RSA

Thanks to the fear of change, it can be agonizing for high achievers to move on from 'good' jobs that no longer feel fulfilling: it means choosing uncertainty and growth over the illusion of safety. But it's the path to a life of greater meaning and joy – and in this wise and generous book, Amina Aitsi-Selmi provides all the encouragement and practical guidance required for making the shift. OLIVER BURKEMAN, WRITER AT THE GUARDIAN, AND AUTHOR, THE ANTIDOTE: HAPPINESS FOR PEOPLE WHO CAN'T STAND POSITIVE THINKING

I believe this book provides an opportunity to reflect on how we can all engage to work together to provide a better future in a volatile, uncertain and complex time. PROFESSOR VIRGINIA MURRAY FRCP, FRCPATH, FFPH, FFOM, HEAD OF GLOBAL DISASTER RISK REDUCTION, PUBLIC HEALTH ENGLAND

In a time of high uncertainty, we have to rethink how we approach our life and our careers. The Success Trap provides valuable insights into how we can all make smart and aligned career (and life) choices in a fast-changing world. DR CHRISTIAN BUSCH, AUTHOR, THE SERENDIPITY MINDSET, AND DIRECTOR, CGA GLOBAL ECONOMY PROGRAM, NEW YORK UNIVERSITY

The Success Trap

*Why good people stay in jobs they
don't like and how to break free*

Amina Aitsi-Selmi

Publisher's note
Every possible effort has been made to ensure that the information contained in this book is accurate at the time of going to press, and the publisher and author cannot accept responsibility for any errors or omissions, however caused. No responsibility for loss or damage occasioned to any person acting, or refraining from action, as a result of the material in this publication can be accepted by the editor, the publisher or the author.

First published in Great Britain and the United States in 2021 by Kogan Page Limited

2nd Floor, 45 Gee Street	122 W 27th St, 10th Floor	4737/23 Ansari Road
London	New York, NY 10001	Daryaganj
EC1V 3RS	USA	New Delhi 110002
United Kingdom		India

www.koganpage.com

Kogan Page books are printed on paper from sustainable forests.

ISBNs

Hardback   978 1 78966 566 6
Paperback 978 1 78966 564 2
eBook   978 1 78966 565 9

British Library Cataloguing-in-Publication Data

A CIP record for this book is available from the British Library.

Library of Congress Cataloging-in-Publication Data

Library of Congress Cataloging-in-Publication Data is available. Control number: 2020042434

Typeset by Integra Software Services, Pondicherry
Print production managed by Jellyfish
Printed and bound by CPI Group (UK) Ltd, Croydon CR0 4YY

*I dedicate this book to my parents, brother,
all my teachers and supporters.*

Contents

Trapping identities: imposter phenomenon and rescuers 45
The rescuer and people pleaser 47
Toxic work myths 51
Learning from the High Achiever Paradox 57

PART TWO
Breaking free from the Success Trap 59

04 Goal-driven versus creative flow 61
The prison of the goal-driven life 62
From rigid goal-setter to creator in flow 70
Creating a new career 78
The bottom line: you're not a machine 81

05 Slow down to speed up 83
The toxicity of constant urgency 84
How to create space 86
Building and maintaining healthy boundaries 92
Resistance to slowing down 96

06 Unlearn your limiting beliefs 101
Resolving the High Achiever Paradox 101
Reality as a psychosocial construct: we mostly make it up 103
Awareness: the key to freedom 104
The High Achiever Paradox Transformation (HAPI)
    process 108
Seven shifts you'll experience with the HAPI process 120

PART THREE
Thriving outside the trap 123

07 Practical freedom: tools to reconnect, respond and
    receive 125
Reconnect: mission, purpose and values 126

About the author

Amina Aitsi-Selmi MD PhD is the Founder and Managing Director of Next Generation Coaching & Consulting Ltd. She's dedicated her 20+ year career to helping individuals and organizations create healthy lives and environments, first as a physician, then as a health policy expert, and currently as an independent specialist consultant and coach.

The depth and breadth of her work with patients, coaching clients as well as global health and policy agencies including the UK Department of Health and the World Health Organization has given her extensive speaking, organizational and educational experience. She's been featured as a World Economic Forum agenda contributor, published over 40 peer-reviewed articles in scientific journals, academic book chapters and policy reports including for the United Nations. Her weekly articles on work culture, leadership and change have received over half a million positive reactions on LinkedIn.

Her diverse range of one-to-one professional coaching clients include doctors, lawyers, accountants, scientists in global organizations spanning intergovernmental agencies and multibillion-dollar companies as well as entrepreneurs. She helps them find freedom where they feel stuck and to move their careers, businesses and lives forward in alignment with their deepest values and with less toxic urgency. Her services also include The Leaders Circle supporting deep conversations as well as speaking on a range of themes in companies and educational institutions like Health Education England and the National Institute of Health and Care Excellence. Themes include dealing with uncertainty, the entrepreneurial mindset, transformational coaching skills and principles of non-violent communication. She has taught graduate students on the social determinants of global health as an Honorary Senior Clinical Lecturer at UCL.

Alongside her medical qualifications and PhD, she's certified in Strategic Intervention from the Anthony Robbins School of Coaching. She's registered with the General Medical Council and is an Affiliate Member of the Institute of Coaching, Harvard Medical School.

Preface
Three questions

I can't say I've ever spent much time in a job I didn't like. It's not that there haven't been ups and downs, but life seems to have been kind in giving me a sense of purpose and bringing the right opportunities. On the other hand, I've had reason to explore the relationship between success and happiness. And I've come to agree with the sages that they are two different things. While there might be a degree of overlap between worldly success and the feeling of achievement, the high moment of success is inevitably followed by a low one, if it isn't treated with some detachment and wisdom.

True happiness, by contrast, seems to be a home within. It's available to the richest and poorest person alike, perhaps more so to the latter, if we go by the biblical adage 'that it is easier for a camel to go through the eye of a needle than for a rich man to enter the kingdom of God'. The idea of the Success Trap – that our past success can get in the way of our future success – may well have biblical support, alongside the mounting scientific evidence and thousands of years of wisdom pointing to our minds as the source of the reality we perceive. The identities, beliefs and myths we unwittingly internalized and that made us so successful in the past, start to hamper our way back home to a deeper happiness.

It's upon realizing that the roller-coaster of success is never ending while happiness is always available, that my career took a different direction, at least to the external observer. From my perspective, this book is the fruit of a lifetime of reflection on the question: 'How can we suffer less and be happier?' It's informed by my career in medicine, health policy, academia and business as well as a lifelong passion for philosophical and spiritual enquiry.

One of the central sociological and ethical questions that I've grappled with since my medical school days and that led to me specializing in big picture health is: 'How much freedom do we truly have?' 'If we are shaped by our environment and the prior conditions that led to our being born into particular circumstances, to what extent are we responsible for our life choices and therefore our happiness?'

I believe these are questions each one of us must find answers to, as they determine the quality of our life experience. Having looked for answers at both ends of the spectrum – the individual (biological and psychological) level with patients and private clients, and the societal structures at local, national and international policy level – I've found that a mind that can answer (or at the very least ponder) these questions satisfactorily functions much better, and its owner is much happier.

In letting go of the tyranny of success as defined by external expectations rather than a deeper wisdom, from both personal experience and working with clients, I've been led to another question: 'How can we be of true service?' After spending 20 years training and working in public service, moving into the private sector as an independent professional seemed anathema to the values I had been grounded in. How can a preoccupation with making money allow for a genuine offer of help? Surely, it would crowd out any honest motive since there would always be an ulterior one?

A few years into the entrepreneurial journey, I came to the conclusion that a preoccupation with any personal motive, whether it be status, advancement or money, will always crowd out a genuine generosity of spirit. This is not a function of working in the public or private sector. It's a function of our level of awareness and whether we are willing to participate in society from a place of generosity and goodwill rather than from fear, anger, scarcity or limitation.

My intention in writing this book is to make an invitation to anyone who feels stuck or trapped in a situation to open up to a new perspective and liberate their true power and essence. Music may be the language of the soul, and writing is a way of making music for the mind. My hope is that this book both uplifts you and challenges your thinking – particularly any limiting beliefs that hold you back from making your fullest contribution. The book doesn't claim to have all the answers and offers an approach to finding out what's on the other side of your perceived limitations.

May you inhabit the freedom and happiness that is every human's birthright while making a difference where you can.

Acknowledgements

I'd like to thank those who have made the book possible including people who supported my earlier career, especially Professor Sir Michael Marmot and Professor Virginia Murray; my coach Rich Litvin for his insights and wisdom; my editor, Rebecca Bush, and Danny Kalman who suggested Kogan Page; all the clients who agreed to share their experience and enriched my understanding for this book; and the friends and family who offered a kind ear, particularly my parents and Edwina Moreton OBE. I'm also grateful for the generous teachings of countless sages throughout the ages, in both East and West, whose wisdom infuses this book.

Introduction

How do you know when to leave your job or change your life?

I had an exploratory coaching conversation with an executive in a tech company once. He'd planned an elegant and detailed exit from corporate life. He felt it was time for something new and didn't even get on particularly well with the executive team or agree with their corporate strategy. But he had a difficult time activating the plan...

I asked him, 'What's stopping you? You've thought about this for a long time and have mitigated all your risks. You've got a great plan for what's next. So what's holding you back?'

He realized: *nothing*.

But he started to hesitate again. He wanted to think about it a bit more. His mind started projecting all sorts of catastrophic scenarios if he resigned. I could sense the self-doubt and a wall of fear rearing itself between him and his big dream.

A few days later, his company was restructured and he was offered an unexpected exit. He told me it was a shock. He was at a loss as to what to do next.

Why do people stay in jobs they don't like?

There are a few different hypotheses on why people stay in jobs they don't like. Many of these ultimately come down to a materialist explanation, along the lines of survival; or rather, the survival of a lifestyle that people want or have to maintain (dream home, private school, nice holidays, etc.). Sometimes a more altruistic motive is evoked, like wanting to have enough money to meet the needs of family and loved ones, especially if they themselves felt deprived in childhood. 'Money isn't everything, but it can make life easier and be a means to do good!' Sound familiar? I think it's more accurate to say that money isn't everything but everyone wants to find out for themselves.

There are also less obviously materialistic explanations, like the desire for respect and a certain status in the professional ranks. The material benefits may be lower, but the intellectual or professional recognition is much higher. Stereotypes of these are the rocket scientist or brain surgeon. From an evolutionary perspective, it's easy to see why we might be biased towards wanting to be at the top of the status ladder. It's safer up there! Social hierarchies also seem to have deleterious effects on health, as I found out during my doctoral research on the global obesity epidemic. Looking plump in an environment where food is seasonal or scarce is a way to mark your status. Transpose that mentality into an era where the food system is flooded with cheap, high calorie foods and you have an obesity epidemic on your hands. It's not just our bodies that can be overfed, our minds can also be overstimulated resulting in chronic anxiety, attention deficit and burnout. But it's hard to see what's happening when the culture and people around you reinforce unhealthy messages of overwork and fear of missing out.

So is it just money, status and safety that are keeping people trapped in jobs? Not necessarily – some cite the socially positive aspects of work, like affiliation, belonging and relationship. So while the job itself may not be fulfilling, the social aspects compensate for that... or at least, the fear of their loss and subsequent isolation act as a deterrent.

Work is part of our human experience. We engage in creative endeavours that produce possibilities for exchange and collaboration and fuel further creativity; we can bring about new discoveries and create new ways of living and experiencing life as humans. Ideally, these work-related endeavours should engage our playfulness as well as our resilience and ability to surmount obstacles. Work can truly offer an opportunity to refine one's character and fulfil one's potential, should one be fortunate enough to encounter the right job, boss and environment.

However, after coaching hundreds of people over more than 1,000 hours around the question of work, purpose and fulfilment, I've been led to conclude the following: why do people stay in jobs they don't like? Because they choose to.

Why we make the choices we make

People sometimes ask me what my coaching method is. My reply is that I don't really have a method. I simply try to understand the world that the person in front of me is caught up in, how they've constructed a worldview that traps them in their current situation, and then help them to find a way back to freedom and fulfilment. They tap into a powerful sense of agency that comes from deep within – not from their fears and basic desires.

Have you ever seen a person make a decision and thought that it didn't make any sense? Well, while a person's decision may not make sense to you, it makes absolute sense to them within their worldview. So a transformational coaching process focused on careers and leadership is a kind of scientific enquiry and a subsequent course correction based on the findings. Biases and errors in a person's thinking and how they weight different aspects of their human experience are examined, misperceptions diagnosed and any fractures with their deepest potential realigned. The realignment of a person's way of thinking or worldview (the mental filter through which they see the world and make decisions) with their deeper potential creates a sense of freedom and vitality. So transformational coaching helps them go beyond the prison they may have inadvertently constructed by questioning the assumptions they believe to be real. As their beliefs transform, so does their life.

This kind of course correction usually requires two things: deep self-enquiry and conversation with a compassionate human being who has gone further than we have. It can be painful to the ego, but a little humility when others point out errors in our thinking can go a long way to learning, unlearning and relearning our basic assumptions. Transformational coaching is a high quality, perspective shifting, heart opening conversation.

Having spent most of two decades working as a doctor on individual- and population-level wellbeing, while spending the majority of my spare time understanding the origins of illness and suffering and how to stop it, I've come to the conclusion that the mental filter through which we view and experience the world is the key to the Success Trap. I've also found that there are three indivisible components to a mental filter that promotes healthy human flourishing rather than stress and feeling stuck. Firstly, the ability to connect to our true home within (awareness); secondly, the ability to ask powerful questions that allow the mind to examine itself (enquiry); thirdly, an awareness of what's going on in our body (energy). We'll come back to these in more detail in Chapter 6.

These three practices have a solid scientific basis as well as being rooted in millennia of contemplative practice. Mindfulness is a practice of bringing a friendly attention to whatever is going on in the moment. You may have come across the enquiry strand under the label 'self-reflection' and the embodied strand under emotional intelligence or somatic practices. Any exercise that makes you more aware of what's going on in your body and how that might be linked to what's going on in your mind is going to expand your level of awareness. In clinical settings, attempts at combining these strands have been made, for example under 'cognitive-behavioural therapy', which has a strong self-reflective component and has been further enhanced with mindfulness approaches to create transformational modalities like mindfulness-based cognitive therapy.

This is great news. Mental health approaches are converging towards the time-honoured questions – if I am not my thoughts, then who am I? And if my thoughts create my reality then how can I engage my thoughts to create a *better* reality? How we live into these questions (not just understand them intellectually but turn insights into action) is a way out of the prison of stress, anxiety and dullness.

How I broke free

Every time I took a career leap in my life to the point I eventually left the beaten track, I had to dig deep using the tools I had gathered through coaching, mindfulness and deep self-exploration as part of my own search for answers. As I moved from hospital doctor, to policy adviser and eventually business owner, I had to somehow find the commitment to stay calm, centred and creative in how I responded to the unique and common challenges in front of me (like how to pay the bills).

It wasn't always pleasant or easy – sometimes it felt like a dark night of the soul – but every time a difficulty was overcome, a mindset shift happened. I felt calmer, clearer and new solutions would emerge as needed.

My aim with this book is to help you understand why we make the choices we do and how we can be free of the fears that trap us in unfulfilling situations so that if you're ever stuck, you'll know what to do to reveal your next step into the unknown and move forward.

How to use this book

The book is designed to take you on a transformational deep-dive like your own personal coaching programme. We start in Part One at high altitude with the global context in which we work in the 21st century. We also look at the types of identities that tend to be rewarded and succeed even if they clash with your deeper potential and true essence as a human (like 'imposter syndrome'). This is the Success Trap.

In Part Two, we start to look at shifting from being mechanically goal-driven to more organic, creative rhythms of performance and what it takes to tap into your inner genius and solve the complex problems at an individual and collective level. You'll discover tools and techniques that help you declutter your mental space and allow for new perspectives and solutions to emerge naturally. This is also where you'll get to practise questioning limiting assumptions that hold you back and do it with patience and kindness so that you can uproot fear at its origin and free your energy and innate genius.

By Part Three, you'll have a good idea of how to break free of the internal structures that hold you back and step out of your habitual patterns of thinking while engaging with the world. We'll look at some tools to capture insights, vision and values as well as communicate with greater presence and leadership. We'll explore how to turn uncertainty into opportunity, the entrepreneurial mindset as an approach to your career and finally how organizations and leaders can help to build a healthier work culture.

The only thing required of you is an open mind and trust that there is more to you than any job or identity.

PART ONE

The Success Trap

Why people stay in jobs they don't like

CHAPTER ONE

The challenge of work in the 21st century

What's wrong with the world of work today? I should start with a caveat: in many ways everything that appears to be wrong has a silver lining. So, admittedly, the question is a flawed one. But for the sake of argument, let's try to investigate what we will call the ailments of the 21st-century labour market.

Let's acknowledge the positive. The global community, rallied under the banner of the United Nations in 2015, formulated its aspirations for a better future for all in the form of the Sustainable Development Goals. In a 2019 review of progress, the United Nations' Secretary General's assessment of goal 8 (that aims for 'decent jobs and economic productivity') was that while labour productivity has increased and unemployment is back to pre-financial crisis levels, 'the global economy is growing at a slower rate. More progress is needed to increase employment opportunities, particularly for young people, reduce informal employment and the gender pay gap and promote safe and secure working environments to create decent work for all' (UN, 2019).

The 2019 World Happiness report shows that material standards of living are the highest they've ever been, but happiness levels do not seem to match up. Across high-income countries, mental health statistics show alarming levels of depression and anxiety. In Europe, fewer than 12 per cent of people report being engaged with their work (Helliwell *et al*, 2019). In a *State of the Global Workplace* report, Gallup found that 85 per cent of employees are disengaged from work, and this amounts to a US $7 trillion loss in productivity. Western countries were among the worst, with only about 10 per cent of employees reporting that they feel engaged with their work (Gallup, 2017). Of course, there may be measurement issues here. However, information collected from tens of thousands of individuals in the UK at different times of the day via a smartphone app, provided millions of bits of data. It shows that paid work is ranked lower in terms of wellbeing than any of the other 39 activities individuals reported engaging in, with the exception of being sick in bed (Bryson and MacKerron, 2017)!

For a more specific insight into the trends around work satisfaction, among UK doctors, one in three GPs is thinking of leaving their job in the next five years (Cook, 2018).

What's going on?

What's wrong with the world of work today?

It would be easy to fill the pages of this book with economic analyses of labour market changes over the past few decades, and discuss quantifiable factors such as stagnant wages, rising costs of living and the impact of these on indicators of wellbeing. If we did, it would not be surprising to discover that paid work has a significant impact on overall life satisfaction and general happiness. This is what economic analyses in the UK, the United States and elsewhere in the world have shown (De Neve and Ward, 2017). Indeed, paid work is a central part of many people's lives. They spend a considerable part of their waking hours doing paid work or seeking paid work if they do not have it.

However, it would be fair to say that while the scientific revolution and the growth of capitalism has dramatically improved our material quality of life and life expectancy, they have failed our deeper existential wellbeing. This is where a social, philosophical and psychological analysis could go deeper into the qualitative, less easily measurable elements of the social fabric of modern society and our human experience of work. After all, as the aphorism goes: *not everything that counts can be measured and not everything that can be measured counts.*

While challenging in its lack of measurability, exploring the human experience is where we can make real gains in collective and individual insights that can change the course of our lives. But first, let's look at the global picture within which we work.

VUCA: Volatile, Uncertain, Complex and Ambiguous

VUCA is an acronym that stands for Volatility, Uncertainty, Complexity and Ambiguity and essentially means: *what the $% &* is going on out there?!* It was first used in 1987, drawing on the leadership theories of the time. Today, it has taken root in theories and ideas related to strategic thinking and leadership in organizations (Bennett and Lemoine, 2014). It has also been used to describe the challenges faced by those organizations; for example, the disruption that can occur from new technologies, political shifts or natural hazards like extreme weather events and infectious diseases.

Here's an example of how VUCA shows up in the organizations that we work for and also in everyday life. In 2011, Thailand experienced some of the worst floods in its history. This brought critical manufacturing factories to a standstill. At the time, the global electronics industry was finally recovering from a massive earthquake in Japan earlier the same year. Thailand serves as an electronics manufacturing hub for hundreds of companies around the world, including the California-based global hard-drive leader at the time. So, the devastating floods had an impact on company operations globally, including through the availability of devices like laptops. In other words, our world is *so interconnected* that the availability of laptops and screens can be affected by the weather on the other side of the globe. The impact of disasters is no longer local – we are all interconnected and vulnerable to the impact of disasters wherever we are, even if the disaster doesn't occur in our own country or region.

HOW VUCA SHOWS UP IN YOUR WORK LIFE

You may have a general sense of decisions being complex at certain points in your career. It's important to remember that there are many factors outside your control and know that any decision involves risk. It's not your responsibility or even possible to figure out the perfect, infallible solution. So, in a sense, you can relax and know that VUCA is inherent to work and careers today. What does VUCA look like for you?

V = Volatility: high speed of change

Example:

In your organization: the stakeholder landscape shifts after a disaster or political upheaval.

In your career: you start a project but it's cancelled or your role is suddenly minimized.

U = Uncertainty: the lack of predictability

Example:

In your organization: a new product or policy is launched that muddies the future of your industry.

In your career: you work towards a career for years that suddenly looks like a dead end.

C = Complexity: the lack of clear cause and effect and the multiplicity of influencing factors in any situation

Example:

In your organization: you work globally and across multiple organizations, each with their own culture, regulations and agendas.

In your career: you get the qualifications, training, networks but still can't make it to the next level or get a promotion in a complicated political landscape.

A = Ambiguity: even if there is a causal chain, it can be misread or misperceived

Example:

In your organization: you expand your remit or market to include an area or audience that you don't know well.

In your career: you spend time and effort developing a strategic relationship only to realize you misread the politics and capabilities.

Artificial intelligence and technological disruption

Much has been said about the radical impact that artificial intelligence (AI) and technological innovation will have on the nature of work. Elon Musk predicts that jobs will be obsolete as robots take over and that we will devote our time to leisure and more complex and fulfilling pursuits – perhaps learning music or enjoying the arts – while receiving a universal wage from the government (Clifford, 2016).

Depending on what kind of job you have, almost half of what you're doing could be automated. One day, you could be job sharing with a robot! A 2017 World Economic Forum report *The Inclusive Growth and Development Report* expressed concern over public services becoming the next Uber and using the gig economy to employ locum doctors and supply teachers (WEF, 2017). A UK report published by Reform proposes that chatbots could replace up to 90 per cent of Whitehall's administrators, as well as tens of thousands in the NHS and GPs' surgeries by 2030, saving as much as £4 billion a year (Hitchcock *et al*, 2017).

McKinsey's research, on the other hand, is more optimistic about our human contribution, and points out that it is not the occupations themselves that will be automated but certain activities within them (McKinsey & Co, 2017). They estimate that today's technology could automate 45 per cent of the activities across all occupations but only 5 per cent of actual occupations. Interestingly, these figures cut across the occupational income ladder and cooks, cleaners, gardeners and carers, who draw on intuitive decision-making and empathy, are more protected from automation than those in high paying positions with a lot of systematic data analysis.

In their book *The Second Machine Age*, Erik Brynjolfsson and Andrew McAfee argue that we're on the verge of the automation of most cognitive tasks, and that software-driven machines will substitute for humans (Brynjolfsson and McAfee, 2014). They believe that digital technologies are doing for human brainpower what the steam engine did for human muscle power at the start of the Industrial Revolution. They also identify three skill areas in which we humans are still far superior to machines:

1 High-end creativity that generates things like great new business ideas, scientific breakthroughs, novels that grip you, and so on.
2 Dexterity, mobility. It's unbelievably hard to get a robot to be a waiter in a restaurant without breaking dishes and terrifying patrons. Sensing and fine manipulation are hard for robots.
3 Emotion, interpersonal relations, caring, nurturing, coaching, motivating, leading.

Whether or not Elon Musk's predictions come to pass, jobs are likely to look significantly different in the next few decades. What does it mean in practice as employees evolve with machine disruptions? Which skills, training and career opportunities should they invest in? The McKinsey & Co survey of 46 countries concludes that all workers will need to adapt as occupations evolve alongside increasingly sophisticated machines. It seems that a reasonable strategy for future workers will be to hone high-level cognitive capabilities including social and emotional skills; creativity (currently the top skill valued by employers (Anderson, 2020)); and other skills that are hard or as yet impossible to automate in solving complex problems of the VUCA world (McKinsey & Co, 2017).

Whatever the future looks like, these changes are certainly forcing us to reconsider the definition of work and what it means to be human. By enquiring into the nature of our human experience and questioning the collectively and individually held beliefs that have been handed down to us, we can start to adapt to the rapid changes that are happening in our work economy and beyond.

The end of careers for life

There are 80,000 hours in a career. That's 40 years × 50 weeks × 40 hours, and arguably a large proportion of your lifetime (80000, 2019)! Last century, it was expected that a career would start with an education or apprenticeship in a relevant field that would lead to gainful employment in a particular field or company, usually until retirement. Today, career change is the norm in many places, including the UK, and most people change careers at least twice (Usborne, 2014). In a survey undertaken by insurance firm Scottish Widows, two-thirds of respondents under 30 were found to have either already made a switch or were planning to do so – and that was in 2014 when the effects of the 2008 recession were still being felt. Contrast that figure with those for people aged over 70: only a third had changed careers at some point (Usborne, 2014).

For many, changing career is not about accumulating wealth, but rather about becoming more self-reliant and fulfilling aspirations. We don't have to fulfil our needs in a hierarchical way (securing our material needs and then our more aspirational needs); we can fulfil them in parallel. We don't 'do well and then do good'. We do well *while* doing good. This makes careers more sustainable in an era where we're expected to work for much longer than previous generations. With longer and less rigid careers, there is uncertainty in the change but also opportunity to fulfil one's full range of career aspirations (Barrett, 2017).

SELF-REFLECTION   Your career

If you spent just 1 per cent of your 80,000 hours in thoughtful, strategic reflection about your work and career, that would be 800 hours. I'm willing to bet most people haven't spent that long! How much time have you spent reflecting on your career and decision-making? Perhaps you've used a traditional approach of discussing it over coffee with a friend or mentor, or over dinner with a partner. Give yourself permission to spend some quality time on this, perhaps even by yourself in a quiet place. You could consider the following:

- Do you enjoy your work?
- What is it that you like about it exactly?
- Can those things be found elsewhere, or are they specific to this job?
- What do you prioritize: safety and remuneration, or meaning and passion?
- If money were no object, what would you do?
- If you had all the meaning and fulfilment in the world, how much would you need to live on?

Our brain in an uncertain world

We can think of the human brain as having two key parts with different modes of operation: 1) the mammalian-reptilian brain, which is responsible for survival, pleasure and avoiding pain; and 2) the neocortex, which is much more recent and able to reason, plan, execute complex tasks and empathize.

The mammalian-reptilian brain is much more ancient in terms of evolutionary history, and as neuroscientists have observed, it has much more power in swaying your behaviour. This is because it triggers powerful physiological responses, which can crystallize into specific emotions like anger or desire. It's very difficult for the more sophisticated and subtle capacities of the neocortex (reasoning, empathy, creativity) to stay engaged when the mammalian-reptilian brain takes over.

If you work in a challenging work culture (excessive competition and aggression), you'll feel justifiably under threat. The combination of our natural human evolution and these factors results in the feeling of being constantly on edge, with the risk of burnout looming. We'll look in more detail at work culture and burnout in the next two chapters. In Part Two we'll explore how we can use our human consciousness superpowers using coaching tools to break through the 'on edge' feeling and recover our optimal and wise decision-making abilities.

Uncertainty as opportunity for reinvention

So now that we've looked at some of what's wrong – what's *right* with the world of work today? The efficiencies permitted by the dominant economic system – namely capitalism – could benefit everyone, especially in conjunction with the checks and balances of the appropriate ethical and regulatory frameworks. And we know that these do work when they are applied. Scandinavia, while having its own challenges, is the often-cited model of an ideal capitalist, social democracy with its high standard of living and egalitarianism.

The defining feature of the globalized system we work in is the expansion of the range of opportunities available. The death of the 'career for life' model has made way for the rise in popularity of relatively new phenomena such as the tech start-up (Apple and Microsoft being among its unicorns of success); and the digital nomad lifestyle in which an entrepreneurial spirit and a willingness to be geographically mobile can lead to exciting and diverse career experiences. However, these opportunities are not equally distributed, and at present, many people struggle to find decent employment, training or decision-making support (let alone 800 hours' worth of self-reflection) to help them navigate the complex labour market of the 21st century. Even for those who do have access to these opportunities, there may be other barriers (external and internal) that stop them from grabbing hold with both hands.

Barriers to career change: the reasons beneath the reasons

In a VUCA world, one can cite any number of reasons for staying put in a job one doesn't like or find fulfilling: the economy, political change, an employers' market, mortgage and school fees that don't pay themselves, etc. While timing and material considerations are very real factors in career decision-making, there is usually a deeper reason to stay. This deeper reason, in my experience, is often informed by a foundational *fear of change*, or an aversion to uncertainty. Having spent thousands of hours in transformational coaching conversations with some of the brightest people in the world, I've developed some understanding of what drives the 21st-century professional. Through deep questions exploring their aspirations and fears around work and life, I've realized this: everyone's choice in the moment makes sense when you look at their reasons for making it. It's the world they've constructed and their choices make sense within it.

Here's an example: say someone is complaining that they're unhappy at work and they're ready for a change. However, they simply don't take any action. They do have some very valid and logical reasons for their inaction: the mortgage, the school fees, timing, the economy, etc. However, there tend to be strategic solutions for each of these practical concerns. So their actions (or inaction) feel incongruent with their stated intention. They want change but don't do anything about it. So they end up stuck between a rock and a hard place. What's going on?

Take my friend, the tech company executive we met in the introduction to this book. He had a beautifully designed exit plan to leave the corporate job that he felt was draining his soul – but for some unknown reason, he just couldn't press the 'go' button. He explained to me that he might be able to do more to help his company; that if he waited, new opportunities might come along to do something more interesting... Eventually, after the company offered him a generous exit package, all of these 'reasons' were removed. It became obvious that what was *really* holding him back was the fear of change and a dislike of the unknown. (There was a happy outcome though – he wrote to me a month later to say that he couldn't believe how good life was on the other side, travelling and spending more time with family!)

The idea that our conscious thoughts are informed by hidden motivators isn't new. Freud famously brought unconscious drives into the psychological conversation and identified repetition compulsion as the mental habit that keeps us trapped in old patterns of thinking and behaviour. Ancient Greek philosophy and Eastern wisdom traditions meticulously explored the human psyche and its contortions over 2,000 years ago. Stoic and Buddhist philosophy may be shrouded in different cultural idiosyncrasies and use different methodologies of enquiry, but they seem to have come to similar conclusions about the human condition. What we can learn from these different schools of thought and philosophy is this:

1 Life can be pretty uncertain, with change being the only certainty. But there are ways of relating to the uncertainty that enable our flourishing rather than imprisonment.
2 Understanding how our mind functions – bringing greater awareness to the source of our thoughts and feelings enables profound resilience and creative responses to whatever circumstances we face.

Essentially, life is uncertain and we can engage with it more healthily through better self-understanding.

The illusion of safety and the Success Trap

We can think of the Success Trap as a materialistic one: where having a particular lifestyle and responsibilities (the rent and the cost of holidays, for example) keep you in a job you don't like very much. While the material aspect may be a factor, the psychological aspect is just as important – and it is here that intervention is possible to help us gain freedom from the trap. Here are three psychological components of the Success Trap:

• the controlling reflex and attachment to old expectations;
• avoiding uncertainty to preserve past gains;
• seeking safety in the wrong places.

Let's unpack these a little further.

The controlling reflex and attachment to old expectations

The psychological aspects of the Success Trap are a kind of illusion: we think that by controlling uncertainty, we will be safe. For example, in the face of a career choice, we may believe that by getting the right education, training or qualifications and the right job, we'll be set. As we've seen in this chapter, this expectation simply isn't realistic in today's world. Refusing to make time and space to examine our relationship to the uncertain with curiosity and compassion keeps us in a controlling reflex that traps us in a less than satisfactory state of affairs. We're attached to how things *should be* or want to return to how things *were in the past* or how they *were for our parents and previous generations.*

Success Trap thinking includes the following expectations:

- secure jobs;
- clear career pathways;
- guaranteed promotion or remuneration;
- small manageable teams;
- clear remits from managers and leaders;
- a pension.

Avoiding uncertainty to preserve past gains

If you are over 30 and have spent a decade in a particular career or lifestyle, you may have reached a point where you feel you have too much to lose. You remember a time when you used to be free and fearless. You remember that you were much happier back then. But now you have too much to lose, so you continue with the job you're not so inspired with. This is called the sunk cost fallacy and it's what keeps you investing in a dead end because you have already invested so much.

Seeking safety in all the wrong places

Have you ever been given dating advice and been told to stop looking for love, especially in the wrong places? Well, there's a career equivalent with searching for safety in all the wrong places. While we can work collectively to create economic and social systems as well as work cultures that promote a sense of safety and belonging, the truth is, we are not quite there yet. But it does not mean you have to struggle or stay trapped going from one draining or mildly satisfying job to the next. Others have taken risks and landed on their feet.

CASE STUDY   A career turning point

A 40-something man comes to see you in your office. He works as a lawyer but is really passionate about politics. He tried his hand at business but it failed and then he tried to run for political office but struggled to get elected. He has a talent for inspiring people but has been told he doesn't have the right education, money or powerful connections for political office. He enjoys his work as a lawyer and is known for his honesty and skill but is wondering whether he should give politics a go again.

You learn that he was born into a modest family and is largely self-educated. His father was a farmer and carpenter. His mother died when he was 9 and he was raised by his sister who died when he was 19. He fell in love, but his sweetheart also died. He eventually married and had three sons, one of whom died recently. His wife complains that he's never at home and doesn't have time for his other children. He's feeling a little low and unsure what to do about his career. Should he stick to the safety of the law or pursue his passion for social change?

What do you say?

Success Trap thinking might say that this man should probably stick to the law, that his disquiet is a result of his recent bereavement and that it's too risky to his family's happiness to pursue another career now. But would you be surprised to learn that this is actually a description of US President Abraham Lincoln?

Abraham Lincoln led the United States through some of its most uncertain times, including the American Civil War. He is credited with preserving the unity of the country, abolishing slavery and modernizing the US economy. But before all that, in the early 1850s, he had settled into practising the law and more or less disengaged from his passion for political change.

Next, let's look at some of the cultural context of the Success Trap in more detail.

CHAPTER TWO

The makings of a career crisis

Career crises are pretty common, at least in Western countries (Robinson and Wright, 2013). According to large economic surveys, most people in the West will experience a crisis of meaning in work and life in their mid-30s. A steady decline in work satisfaction seems to ensue and hit a nadir in the mid-50s, before starting to rise again after that, resulting in a U-shape in work satisfaction over a person's career (Schwandt, 2015). Research from over 500,000 Americans and Western Europeans showed a parallel pattern in terms of happiness and wellbeing: a decline in the 30s, hitting rock bottom in the mid-50s then rising again (Blanchflower and Oswald, 2008). Interestingly, this pattern is present in high-, low- and middle-income countries and didn't discriminate by socioeconomic level. It affected white-collar workers, blue-collar workers, married people and single people alike.

It is not clear which comes first (the life crisis or the career crisis), but the good news is that if you're going through a crisis in your career or life, it is likely to improve steadily after your mid-50s. On the other hand, a watch and wait approach might not feel very appealing, particularly if you know that you could alter the course of the crisis and turn it into an opportunity.

Crisis or opportunity

We now understand more than ever how the mind and the brain work – so a *laissez faire* approach of 'wait and see' seems a little feeble and fatalistic! The role of integrated psychological approaches in incorporating mindfulness and other somatic and reflection tools in our lives, as well as enabling skilful action to improve life, work and relationship circumstances, can't be ignored. If someone is beginning to sense a lack of alignment between their career and their values, the healthy response would be to take the time and space, and use the appropriate tools and skills, to examine the misalignment. The career crisis then becomes an opportunity: an opportunity to re-evaluate your criteria for decision-making, your priorities, your values and make a considered assessment of opportunities going forward.

However, this kind of intervention is not routinely offered, except in organizations where a coaching culture and a willingness to invest in staff exists. Others leave individuals to their own devices. From a medical point of view, withholding an intervention available is unethical and potentially criminal. Yet, this is what's happening in many workplaces and organizations today.

CASE STUDY Xena

Xena was a highly competent doctor specializing in big picture health policy and research. She had worked for a number of years with government and with a range of national and international organizations. By all accounts she was an accomplished, service-driven professional with a bright future ahead of her. She was doing the work she had dreamt of years before. However, she was starting to feel a misalignment between her need for autonomy and creativity and the more regimented and hierarchical culture around her. She was also starting to doubt herself and wondered whether her contribution was valuable. There was a sense she might be missing something. Did she need to work harder or gain more leadership training and communication skills? Was it time to look in a new direction? Was there a way of moving up the ladder with integrity so that she didn't compromise her values in the competition for more senior roles? How could she even begin to discover the answers to such questions that are both personal and ethical?

Why do career crises happen?

Xena's situation is not uncommon. But at the individual level, the causes are not always clear immediately. Why does a career and life that one worked towards for decades suddenly feel empty and draining? Why does it tend to happen in the mid-30s? What is the relationship to the wider work environment and why do things spontaneously improve in the mid-50s?

Outside of the VUCA context of work in the 21st century that we looked at in the first chapter, it's been suggested that life stages may be a factor. In other words, in the mid-30s, dashed hopes and the sense that one will never fulfil one's full potential is a factor for dissatisfaction, while in the mid-50s contemplation of mortality leads to a reconciliation with reality and a desire to make the most of life (Schwandt, 2015). Another possibility is that the mid-30s is a perfect intersection of accumulated career and life capital and creative life energy. For example, while it may seem like the early 20s are the best time to start a business, data suggest that people over the age of 35 are more likely to start a business and succeed at it because they've had time to clarify their values and mission as well as having better career and financial capital to set the business going (Gallo, 2018). Other reasons include:

- Personal: we may reach a point where our values and preferences change. Perhaps you start a family and want to cut back on relentless work commitments or feel it's time to write that novel and create more space through more flexible consulting work.
- Societal: careers for life are ending. So it's only natural to reach a point where a change begins. The jobs we started in may no longer be relevant or meaningful; for example, if an algorithm or a machine is able to perform better and more safely than a human brain and the qualities that make us uniquely human are better used elsewhere.
- Universal: humans are living for much longer, so we have much more time to evolve and express more of our capacities and gifts. Compared to our ancestors, we can live two or three lifetimes and change facilitates our species' evolution!

The good thing about a career crisis is that often, once we get over the shock of our real limitations (ageing, disease and death), we can discover a motivation to remove all of our self-imposed and psychological limitations. In other words, it's a normal and healthy event in life. While a career crisis has a positive side, it's worth acknowledging its darker aspects for a moment, especially in light of the increasingly complex and heavy workloads of the VUCA world.

Burnout

There is no universally agreed upon definition of burnout (Korczak and Huber, 2012). However, links have been made between burnout and feelings of entrapment. In theory, entrapment happens when people feel stuck in their work. They are less attracted to what they're doing every day, but they feel they have to stay because:

- they perceive a lack of attractive alternatives;
- they believe they have too much invested to quit;
- they think others expect them to continue with it (Raedeke *et al*, 2000).

When I practised medicine, I was well aware of the effect that diagnostic labels like 'burnout' had on patients. On the upside, they had a name for their symptoms and the uncertainty around the illness was a little easier to bear. On the downside, it created a new identity in the form of a person who fits the 'patient role'. Labels can have a powerful effect, even if they're just a concept or name that someone gave to a collection of symptoms. The label creates a risk of keeping the person victimized and fostering feelings of powerlessness that deprive them of their internal resources to recover from the 'illness'. All along the person's inner wisdom may have been suggesting solutions.

For the purpose of this book, we'll define 'burnout' as a result of a (career) crisis that has been ignored. In other words, it's the result of ignoring the inner signals, or your own intuition telling you that you need to take a step back and re-evaluate your situation. While burnout is often associated with the idea of working too hard, it is also the result of working on the wrong thing. It might not just be about overdoing it; it might be that you're working in a way or in a job that isn't right for you (Mayo Clinic, 2018).

The truth about burnout

By all accounts, work processes – the means by which we turn human energy into things or outputs – are faster and more efficient today than they have ever been. We saw this in Chapter 1. Sociologists have coined the term 'the fourth industrial revolution'. The harnessing of steam, electricity, automation and now digital technology between the 19th and 21st centuries has radically transformed the way human labour is used and how things are produced (Schwab, 2016). The speed of current breakthroughs has no historical precedent. From an individual perspective, we experience this as pressure to adapt (a kind of natural selection), perform and produce, often with fewer resources (financial and psychological) than previous generations as budgets are squeezed, no one has time and sources of wise guidance are few.

One of the advantages of speed, from an economic perspective, is that today, we're more efficient at transforming a kilojoule of human energy into a product that can be exchanged.

What's wrong with that?

Nothing as such, unless we look at the impact on our relationship with:

- ourselves (in how we see ourselves as humans both in identity and essence);
- each other (the relationships that make up the social fabric we're embedded in);
- our environment (in how we relate to – or exploit – nature).

These fast and efficient processes seem to separate us from our creativity and our ability to relate deeply with objects and people. They seem to distance us from nature, the source of everything, and the deeper social fabric. By virtue of the increased speed of work in the VUCA world, our cognitive processing abilities appear to be increasingly overwhelmed, our attention split and our energy scattered. This makes it difficult to have a holistic experience of life: if we are overwhelmed and scattered, it is much more difficult to feel whole.

So, while burnout refers to an individual phenomenon for which we need individual-level solutions, the truth is that burnout is closely linked to wider, systemic phenomena that are outside any individual's control. The only factor we do have control over is how we choose to interact with the system.

Because of the role of the wider context, some psychologists have questioned whether the term 'burnout' is actually a misnomer. Instead, it's been argued that burnout is a result of repeated and unsustainable compromise of one's deeply held values – like justice, wellbeing or compassion. Therefore, if a person is in a situation where they are forced into the repeated and unsustainable compromise of their values – how they see themselves, others and the world – then what we call 'burnout' is not an individual failing or an individual problem. It is something done to you, not by you – and so, by some, burnout has been relabelled as 'moral injury' (Norman and Maguen, 2020). And so, if burnout is redefined as a systemic problem, then it requires a systemic solution. In the meantime, what we do at individual level has a ripple effect.

Why is burnout hard to stop?

While a full-blown episode of burnout or exhaustion is unmistakable, the build-up to it can be insidious, especially for people who are disconnected from their intuition and ignore their need for rest and relaxation. But this isn't just down to individual level factors, as we've seen. The environment or culture we live and work in may exacerbate this disconnection, by encouraging a 'do or die' mentality where individuals plough on and ignore their emotional, psychological and physical needs; or through a constant stream of information and interactions leading to an inability to switch off.

There's one situation where this hard push may be appropriate: when you're in a pure survival situation. If you're being chased by a sabre-toothed tiger, your higher needs are switched off. There's no time to worry about justice, connection or even minor injuries – you just run and keep going or turn around and fight for your life. Unfortunately, even though being chased by hungry sabre-toothed tigers is no longer a primary concern in our society, our work culture and psychology still carry remnants of this quality of survivalism.

Individuals frequently experience survival-like physiological responses to everyday work activities, like an important meeting, interview or managing conflict. Public speaking in particular can provoke intense fear (Dwyer and Davidson, 2012). For our bodies and brains, it's easy to confuse everyday trials and tribulations with a survival issue. As you can imagine – or may have experienced for yourself – being constantly in survival mode is pretty tiring and unsustainable. Tension accumulates in the body and it starts to break down. But because it feels like a survival issue, we keep going on that project, strategy, job or career until we drop.

Survival mission creep

If you've ever worked on a project, you'll know that one of the dangers is an ambiguous scope, leading to what project managers call 'mission creep'. The tasks and expectations of the project keep growing with no end in sight, because there are no clear limits to the activity – so you end up with moving goalposts and endless activity. Expectations, left unmanaged, tend to grow without stopping.

This is what seems to happen with our survival mechanism in the modern world. No amount of material or psychological gain is enough! There is always more to own, more to earn and more to learn! Of course, it's not that any of these things are inherently wrong or bad, but when these moving goalposts become a survival issue, the body and mind are unable to relax and enjoy the present, and they become counter-productive to a sense of happiness and fulfilment.

However, happiness studies have shown that endless gain does not lead to happiness (Jebb *et al*, 2018). Whenever you get something you want, you're happy for a while then return to your default happiness level. So it can feel like the only way to sustain the uptick in happiness is to keep chasing one thing after the next. It's been called the 'hedonic treadmill' (Layard, 2011).

Why doesn't higher income always lead to greater happiness or emotional wellbeing? Well, higher incomes are usually accompanied with higher pressure and demands (time, workload, responsibilities) that might also limit opportunities for fulfilling experiences including intimate relationships and creative endeavours. Other factors may play a role in increasing stress despite greater income, such as stronger materialistic values, additional material aspirations that may go unfulfilled, increased social comparisons or other life changes resulting from greater income; for example, having more children or living in more expensive neighbourhoods (Barr, 2018).

But the craving for more money or status can be hard to deactivate if you're on the hedonic treadmill. Grasping onto material possessions and status for comfort and safety is pretty much a reflex of the human mind, as we saw in the last chapter. When we are born, we are afraid of two things: loud noises and being dropped. Babies have a grasping reflex that disappears after a few months. However, it may take a lifetime to let go of our grasping reflex towards material possessions and status. It may take an episode of burnout or crisis to help us wake up. The good news is a crisis can be turned into an opportunity to step back, self-assess and consider new possibilities with more freedom. With an open mind and commitment, you can work on your happiness set point to create a new default rather than grasp at objects or status to create fleeting moments of happiness. We'll turn to tools and techniques that can help in Part Two.

Toxic work cultures: the collective trap

About three years into my 2016 career leap from a highly structured and competitive career into something more entrepreneurial and fluid, I started really noticing the contrast in my daily experience of work. By that point, I'd spent about a thousand hours coaching successful professionals who were re-evaluating and sometimes pivoting their career trajectory – and I was seeing the commonalities with increasing clarity.

For example, Xena was clear that one of her core values was autonomy and that she didn't do well in environments that were highly controlling or prescriptive. Her ability to creatively synthesize complex information and communicate it effectively in high pressure, high complexity environments seemed under-used. She enjoyed many aspects of her work – it was meaningful, prestigious, well-paid and she had the opportunity to travel, meet fascinating people and engage in the global conversation – but she felt trapped in a culture that did not quite align with her values with no hope of things improving. There were no obvious avenues for progress without significant compromise and it wasn't easy to articulate the sense of unease without coming across as difficult or contrarian.

What is a toxic work culture?

You've probably come across an environment that you would describe as toxic. You might think of an environment where competitiveness dominates (people hog credit, talk over one another, devalue each other to improve their own standing, claim superior knowledge through snide criticism, etc.) – you have to watch your back as you inch your way up the pole of power and status. There's a constant sense of threat and manipulative politicking. You may also feel a shortage of resources and of having to do more with less.

There are three work-related psychosocial factors that are well known in scientific research to be linked to negative health and wellbeing outcomes, including death, heart disease, diabetes, mental illness and burnout (Joubert and Rothmann, 2007; Marmot, 2015) plus one more that is harder to measure but no less significant. Any one of these factors is enough to create what we can call a 'toxic' work culture – but in many toxic workplaces, you are likely to see at least two or more at play. These are:

- job strain;
- effort–reward imbalance;
- rigid hierarchy;
- dysfunctional competition.

Job strain

You have a high workload with little control over it, ie a lack of autonomy under stressful conditions. This has been shown to lead to 'learned helplessness' and is linked to several mental and physical illnesses.

Effort–reward imbalance

You work hard and put a lot of energy and commitment in, but the salary, promotion prospects, job security, esteem and recognition don't match up. Again, that eventually causes stress and illness.

Rigid hierarchy

Rigid hierarchies can be described as a social order that gives different levels of access to resources like money, power and connections. It has been shown that being lower down in the hierarchy (for example, in a work setting), leads to a higher risk of health problems, for example in the extensive Whitehall studies led by Professor Michael Marmot at UCL (Marmot, 2015). What's more, the sense of being lower in the pecking order harms everyone's health relative to the person at the top. While rigid hierarchy can be useful in war situations where command-and-control style organization is helpful to manage a crisis effectively, it is less helpful in the volatile and complex world we live in today. In most work contexts, innovation and collaboration are more effective qualities (IBM, 2010).

Dysfunctional competition

This factor is less well understood, because it's harder to measure. Systems that pit individuals against each other, in order to squeeze productivity gains and push people to perform harder, may be the most damaging of all – if current research on psychological safety is anything to go by (Edmonson, 2018). In the 12-step programme, you're advised not to make decisions if you're Hungry, Angry, Lonely or Tired (HALT). Yet how many of us keep going at work, despite feeling any or all of these at once? Leaders may do much better in measuring people's work by the value they produce rather than the hours they put in (Schwartz, 2010). Strong, rational and empirically informed arguments are increasingly made that leaders who help their employees feel safe, valued and appreciated are the most needed (Sinek, 2017).

Why do we stay in toxic work cultures?

You've probably heard people say that it's just how the world works. Humans are greedy and flawed and we just have to survive the best we can. It's a dog eat dog world out there. But these ideas, while arguably based on realities of our human history, also get in the way of change. It's not a helpful thing, if you're feeling stuck, to fatally believe that this is just the way things are. More than that, we reinforce toxic culture by believing in its origin myths.

So what is the alternative? If it's not down to individual flaws, fear or greed, then what keeps people in a work trap?

Much of the toxic corporate culture that squeezes human capital for profit is based on wider factors beyond any one person's control, as we saw in Chapter 1. Capitalism as a system has its problems. The fact that a small elite owns the means of production, while the majority exchange their labour for money, creates an imbalance of power. Then, those who own the means of production – for example, the shareholders in a company – are likely to choose leadership and management structures that align with their own values and interests.

For example, the theory of shareholder value maximization, which emerged in the 1980s, prioritizes shareholder payouts and therefore company profit (rather than social value or staff well-being). This means that executives and management teams are often put in place to do just that – maximize profit for share-holders at all costs. In the end, this approach is arguably damaging organizations, employees and wider society (Stout, 2012). It's not a universal law, of course. Exceptions do exist. But by understanding the historical origin of our current work culture, we can hopefully change it by re-evaluating its usefulness.

Systems that trap and dysfunctional competition

With these wider factors in mind, let's now focus on what is within our control. At an individual level, we can look at the people, places and habits that create a sense of stress, tension or entrapment, and evaluate where we can intervene. This is how you can regain a sense of agency and freedom.

INCENTIVES THAT TRAP
Big bonuses and promotions based on how much money we make for an organization or company will, of course, skew our behaviours away from a people focus. Getting the bonus will also keep us in the race for the next big bonus and fund a life-style that we'll find difficult to let go of. A particularly insidious form of this is known as 'golden handcuffs': this describes a set-up where benefits and deferred payments are provided by an

employer to discourage you from taking employment elsewhere. You are literally paid to stay. Less tangible incentives are the validation given to those who 'get results' rather than care for their team. These demonstrate the unhealthy habits of working late and at the weekend, and responding to emails at all hours of the day. The implicit approval of these behaviours can make it hard to escape.

BOSSES THAT TRAP

Bosses are supposed to be people we look up to. They have power and authority and so we're likely to pay attention to what they say. If they're sold on the profit-driven work culture, it's likely they'll reinforce these messages for you. At worst, they might bully you or heighten your sense of insecurity so that you're less likely to entertain alternatives (Sinek, 2017). The 'Great Man' theory of leadership has been espoused for most of the last century, and holds that great achievements are the result of a single man's efforts rather than a group or system. Needless to say that in trying to live up to this, many bosses have created toxic atmospheres where everything is centred around them and other people's needs are ignored.

COLLEAGUES THAT TRAP

We are empathic creatures by nature, and we pick up on other people's moods and thoughts. Over time, we can be at risk of making them our own. Engaging in negative talk, backbiting and gossiping with unhappy colleagues can bring your positivity down and drain your energy away from things that you really want.

SUCCESS MYTHS THAT TRAP

We've looked at some of these already; for example, that more money, more status and more possessions equate to happiness and success. It simply is not true, but these myths keep us on the treadmill.

WORK MYTHS THAT TRAP

Many old ideas around productivity and loyalty are out of date for the fast-moving world of work today. Some of these include:

- idle hands are the devil's workshop (you must stay busy);
- hate the game, not the player (you must play the game/the politics);
- time is money (money is a priority);
- eat what you kill (in finance);
- publish or perish (in academia).

Much of this kind of work ethic is thought to have religious origins, coming from the protestant Christian belief that working hard was a sign of being among those predestined for paradise (Weber and Swedberg, 2009).

We'll look at some of these work myths in more detail in Chapter 3.

SELF-REFLECTION   Work myths

What are some of the work myths you've grown up with?

How old were you when you picked these up?

Are you ready to let go of those that don't serve you anymore?

IDENTITIES THAT TRAP

We can adapt so well and become so habituated to a certain work culture or set of myths that we inhabit a certain way of being or create a personality that is hard to shake off. Our surroundings almost become a part of our identity – some might call it institutionalization. Your habits become your destiny. In the next chapter we'll look in more detail at some of these.

Breaking out

So what did Xena choose? The road less travelled or sticking it out? Through reflection and enquiry, she realized that despite her success and job security, she wasn't true to her values and living this way in pursuit of some eventual resolution was exhausting. She concluded that climbing the career ladder would require compromise that she was not willing to make. Fortunately, she met a leader in her field who shared her vision and values and offered her a new set of opportunities with global organizations working on key issues. She experienced a renewed fulfilment in work, support for her creativity as well as an encouragement and respect for her autonomy that felt appropriate for her stage of career. She remembered what it was like to feel excited about the work she was doing. During this time, she realized that what she really wanted was more freedom and space to work on her own terms, with more flexibility and more time for family, friends and creative expression. She also sensed that true security and safety started with her own abilities and that another way of working was possible. Like the majority of people who step into entrepreneurship and business she was ready to become her own boss (Simovic, 2019).

She stepped into work as an independent professional and arranged her life into something that matched more closely her inner rhythms and values. She was able to travel, spend more time with family and rest as much as she needed. She tapped into her creativity as she grappled with the uncertainty of independent work, finding her way one step at a time.

Career changes are not uncommon and the 'career for life' model appears to be coming to an end (Usborne, 2014; Fleming, 2019). But it's less common for women to set up a business in the UK where statistics lag behind other countries like Canada, Australia, the United States and a number of European countries. The percentage of women engaged in entrepreneurship in the UK in 2017 was 5.6 per cent compared to 15 per cent in Canada and 11 per cent in the United States (Rose, 2019). In Part Three we'll explore how to shift from being an employee to adopting an entrepreneurial mindset and how to apply that to your career even if you work within an organization.

Here's the key lesson learned from my own transition: I know that I could not have completed the transition into a new phase of my career based on the set of habits of thought patterns that made me successful earlier in my career. I strongly believe that letting go of the need to control the outcome through planning and/or the need for certainty by trying to find the right answers were major mindset shifts. When I developed the willingness to deal with ambiguity and take risks, the path unfolded. I'm increasingly convinced, both from my own experience as well as the conversations I've had with hundreds of professionals and entrepreneurs, including my coaching clients, that our work is not to force dreams to happen, but instead to remove the barriers to their unfolding.

So, we've seen that career (and mid-life) crises are common – it's nothing to feel odd about if you're going through it or just contemplating your options. Many factors are outside your control. Cultural factors like unhelpful expectations about success have a role. However, ignoring your own intuition or inner-signals that something isn't quite right can prolong a crisis unnecessarily, when it can be turned into an opportunity to step back, connect to your deeper values and develop the courage to live in alignment with what really matters to you.

In the next chapter, we'll look in more detail at the individual experience of the Success Trap. We'll explore how high achievers while being paragons of competence in the culture are at a disadvantage in terms of breaking out of the Success Trap – what we might call the High Achiever Paradox.

CHAPTER THREE

The High Achiever Paradox, imposter syndrome and other work identity traps

The idea that those who succeed in terms of education, occupation and income might eventually be at a disadvantage in terms of mental health, happiness and fulfilment is not necessarily an intuitive one. This is what I call the High Achiever Paradox – winning the race and losing happiness – and it is a huge factor in the Success Trap.

We've explored the global, social and organizational context of the Success Trap, and now it's time to look more closely at our own individual thought patterns and behaviours. Following the ideas in this Part, you'll be in a great position to use the transformational tools in Part Two to help you break out of any success trap and free yourself to create an experience of deeper fulfilment in work and life.

The High Achiever Paradox

What do you do after you've won the rat race...?

CASE STUDY   Diana

When Diana and I met in 2016, she felt overwhelmed by work. Here she was, a newly minted hospital consultant in one of the most competitive medical specialties, with ambition matched only by her father's enormous success in the same specialty. Working in a busy city hospital, she felt she had no time to develop her career for the next level – and that her personal life needed attention too. She hoped coaching would help her create a career in a different city, in a different hospital, with more autonomy. She wanted more intellectual challenge and inspiration, to work on exciting projects that allowed her to make a real contribution. She hoped to lead her own hospital service – just like her father. Finally, she wanted a healthy and meaningful relationship with someone special, as well as reconnecting with her creativity – and she had multiple creative talents.

Within a few months after we started working together, Diana was sought after by the top hospitals in the country. She was offered leadership of her own service in one of the country's most prestigious hospitals, which she took up. She was quickly recognized for her work through national excellence awards and was invited to speak at international conferences. She met a wonderfully caring and understanding partner whom she enjoys travelling with and is creating a family with. She ran half-marathons regularly and revived creative hobbies.

Three years to the day, her dream had come true!

But, eventually, she started to feel restless again. She wondered whether she was not doing enough, or doing too much, or doing the wrong thing altogether. I've been there too. And it's overwhelming. Sure, some time management and prioritization could help a bit... But the truth is that with the High Achiever Paradox, challenges, goals and success become your way of living and it's hard to unhook.

While it's great to get to the top of a mountain, you inevitably have to come back down. If you're not careful, you feel happy only when climbing the mountain. And so you keep having to find the next mountain to climb. In Buddhist philosophy, this never-ending cycle of beginnings and endings is called *samsara*. You may have noticed yourself that the satisfaction of achievement never lasts very long before a new desire for something to fill up your time and absorb your attention arises. The good news is that we have a chance to free ourselves and find deeper fulfilment.

The High Achiever Paradox means you're good at climbing 'mountains' – but you're unable to enjoy the process fully or feel satisfied for very long. As you start succeeding at climbing mountains, you develop a taste for it. But you hate coming down from the mountain and feel restless when you're at the bottom or between mountains. The more mountains you climb, the more you realize it will never bring you the true fulfilment you seek. You start to notice that:

- Your schedule is always packed.
- You feel restless and have trouble relaxing/sleeping.
- You're often looking for the next challenge.
- Your personal life or self-care takes a back seat easily.
- You get a high from fixing a problem or reaching a goal, which fades quickly.
- Failure is unfamiliar.

You don't notice that you're always performing.

SELF-REFLECTION   High achiever traits

How many of the traits listed above do you experience?

If you could focus on one of these as an area for transformation in the next 12 months, which would it be?

If we're not careful, we can become like the mythical Sisyphus, constantly rolling the boulder up a hill only to have it roll back down and start all over again. Psychoanalyst and pragmatic philosopher Erich Fromm summed it up thus: 'like a ghost: it leaves us disappointed as soon as we believe we have caught it – the illusory happiness called success' (Fromm, 2001).

Why a career crisis can feel worse if you're a high achiever

There is nothing inherently problematic with being a high achiever. The negative aspect of achievement, like any habit of thought or behaviour, is when it becomes *compulsive*. One of the compulsions behind achievement is the need to win (which is why failure can feel so painful). Everything becomes a competition and life becomes a strategy that can be optimized – it's about survival rather than flourishing. It's about how much you can take rather than how much you can create. As a result, opportunities, health and relationships can suffer.

If you've been rewarded for certain skills and talents that landed you in a particular career, it takes a lot of courage to start questioning whether it is truly the path for you. Echoing the observation of Harvard political philosophy professor, Michael Sandel, if you happen to have skills and talents that society values, you'll be rewarded for your performance from a young age (Sandel, 2020). Achieving becomes your way of living. But you had no real choice in the matter to start with.

Wanting to make a change to your work or life because you feel like you've failed for some reason is one thing. You can put it down to bad luck, learn from the experience and eventually get back in the saddle. You may need some help or some time to recover, but you'll find the motivation again. On the other hand, feeling successful but that something still isn't right is quite another. It brings another set of psychological and emotional challenges. Guilt is a big one. Loss of everything you've built in life is another. And facing the unknown of what it all means for the future is possibly the most paralysing of all. It takes great courage to leave a successful situation and follow a completely new direction with no guarantees you'll ever be 'successful' again.

These are psychological challenges that high achievers face when they start to feel trapped. I've coached a good number of high achievers (successful doctors, lawyers, scientists and organizational leaders in the UK and internationally) and the guilt factor is probably the most confusing. Take doctors, for example, they are traditionally well respected and command high status. There's a lot of social value, meaning and intellectual stimulation in their work, and it's often well paid. It hits the sweet spot or Ikigai of work (a Japanese term for *purpose* in life, which we'll revisit in Chapter 7). So, when they start to question their path, a sense of ingratitude surfaces. This can be compounded if your family has invested a lot of time, energy and resources in providing you with the education and support you needed to succeed in this particular career. So not only can it feel confusing to be dissatisfied in this ideal job, the guilt towards others who supported you and have high expectations of you can be crippling.

In other words, if you're a high achiever in that sense, you can easily feel *guilty* about your career crisis. You might be ashamed of wanting to leave a job or career that others would do anything for. Perhaps it gives you security, and your family invested so much for you to get there. The job situation looks good on the outside, relatives and bosses may want you to stick with it, but deep inside, you are deeply unhappy. Your socially validated success and your talent for the job are in the way of your true fulfilment.

Trapping identities: imposter phenomenon and rescuers

One of the most important ingredients of intentional transformation of your career or life is readiness for change (Sampson *et al*, 2000). It will help you to weather the obstacles – the limiting beliefs and identities you hold about yourself as well as factors outside your control. While the research on high achiever psychology isn't that extensive outside of sports psychology, we do have other overlapping concepts and identities: imposter syndrome and the rescuer identity. So let's look at these.

Imposter phenomenon

Closely related labels to the high achiever or overachiever are 'workaholic' and 'imposter syndrome'. Imposter syndrome – originally termed imposter phenomenon – is probably the most recognizable label with some statistical evidence available. Imposter feelings are not uncommon: one UK survey found that 85 per cent of UK adults admitted to feeling inadequate or incompetent at work, and almost 70 per cent don't feel they deserve their current success (TheHubEvents, 2019).

One of the original studies in the 1970s looked at a group of successful women academics and professionals (Rose *et al*, 1978). Despite their prestigious degrees, high achievement on standardized tests, praise and professional recognition from colleagues and respected authorities, they still felt like frauds. It was hypothesized that, for some reason, they were unable to internalize any kind of success. People who've reported feeling like imposters include Maya Angelou, Meryl Streep, Michelle Obama and Neil Armstrong.

Some of the beliefs they held were:

- I'm not intelligent.
- I have fooled those who think I am intelligent.
- My success/results/grades are because of an error in other people's judgement.

- I'm not really qualified to do this role.
- Someone will find out I'm a phony/fraud eventually.
- If I don't get this job/promotion/role/place, I'll be relieved.

They also tended to say that they felt anxious or depressed and suffered from a lack of self-confidence a lot of the time, as well as frustration in meeting self-imposed standards of achievement. In short, they experienced a lot of self-doubt. In response to tasks or deadlines, one of two responses tended to occur: 1) procrastination initially and then going all out as the deadline approached; or 2) working really hard throughout. In either case, success was not attributed to their own ability: it was either a fluke or due to hard work rather than any gifts or talents they may have. In essence, they made it impossible to feel good about themselves! They were their own worst enemy.

It's not entirely clear what causes imposter phenomenon. Ultimately, it will have the same complex causes as any trait or habit of thinking and behaving: it's a mixture of the myths and narratives we picked up from others, and the natural human need to belong and feel safe. At some point, you may have started believing that you needed to prove yourself to be accepted. There appears to be a link between how you were identified as a child and imposter feelings in adult life. There is a higher risk if you were called one of these (Hoang, 2013):

- 'The smart one';
- 'The talented one';
- 'The responsible one';
- 'The sensitive one';
- 'The good one';
- 'Our favourite'.

If you have recognized yourself in any of the above and feel there's a link, you may be wondering what you can do about it. Well, the first step is awareness – recognizing that you may have been too harsh on yourself and that there may be other identities for you to inhabit. You may also recognize that the work culture around you might reward your self-doubt to get you to perform, and that this is ultimately not sustainable for you. Speaking about what you're noticing and realizing that you're not crazy or alone in these patterns, starts to break them up and give you more freedom to choose different thoughts and behaviours going forward.

SELF-REFLECTION   Trapping core beliefs

Spend a moment (or a few days) noticing your thoughts. Do any of these come up regularly?

- I'm not good enough.
- I must work harder.
- I don't want to let anyone down.
- I don't want people to think I'm weak.
- I have to do everything myself.

Notice when and where these thoughts come up. Are there particular people, situations or places that trigger them?

The rescuer and people pleaser

Like imposter phenomenon, rescuer syndrome is not a clinical entity or disease. They are both concepts used in psychology to capture some of the patterns of thought and behaviour that lead people to sabotage their own potential while meaning to help others. Similar concepts and labels include white knight syndrome, hero/heroine complex and martyr complex. A close relative is the people pleaser.

Rescuer syndrome has been documented to have serious life-and-death consequences. Accidental drowning remains a leading cause of death among children. A disproportionately large percentage of deaths has been found to occur among those who dive in to save the drowning child. They save the child but drown themselves. These rescuers are often a parent or relative who acts impulsively. Of course, the notion of self-sacrifice is noble and no one could say that they wouldn't do the same. However, if there was a way to save the child without the rescuer dying themselves, wouldn't that be better? It is thought that many of these rescuer deaths could be prevented through better awareness of drowning risks and learning a range of life-saving skills, for example (Franklin and Pearn, 2011).

Here's another example: if you've ever been on a flight, you may have heard the message to *put your oxygen mask on first* before helping anyone else. As you can imagine, if you're with a child, your altruistic instinct might be to put the oxygen mask on the child first. However, your awareness drops surprisingly rapidly and unexpectedly when you're deprived of oxygen. The risk then is that your child is left without a parent to attend to them in a situation of major danger, not to mention that no one may be able to attend to you if you lose consciousness. NASA released a video demonstration of what a lack of oxygen does to your judgement and how rapidly it occurs to help people understand the importance of this principle (Coffey, 2017).

Of course, these behaviours are not limited to parents and are documented in the workplace, particularly in the helping professions and among leaders. The problem isn't the helping instinct in itself. Offering help is a good thing! However, it becomes a problem when 'helping' becomes a compulsion, one that doesn't consider all angles of the situation like in the drowning scenario above (Kets de Vries, 2012). In addition, helping at the wrong time or place can deprive the person you're trying to help of their own problem-solving abilities and they may learn to be helpless. Over time, this can become one-sided behaviour and result in an energy drain. Often, the 'rescuer' is oblivious to these negative impacts, because they're focused on the positive feelings that come from rescuing and the validation that comes from pleasing. They become addicted to the feelings of pleasure, significance or momentary connection that come from helping – a *helper's high*, if you will. A related manifestation is the addiction to praise and validation – the *disease to please*.

Inevitably, these identities are a risk factor for compassion fatigue, resentment and burnout. A High Achiever Paradox can manifest here, since the better you become at rescuing, advising and fixing, the more problems will be presented to you. You unwittingly become the go-to person whenever there's a problem or crisis. Saying 'no' becomes difficult because it clashes with your identity as the one who can fix everything. We'll look at how to break out of this in more detail in Part Two.

Ten signs you may be a rescuer

The challenge with changing patterns that aren't helpful is that we can't see our blind spots. In my work, I have seen some common signs that people with 'rescuing' behaviour tend to show.

1 **Your job may reflect your rescuer identity**

    You may be a doctor or a nurse, or work in the charity sector. In the private sector, you will tend to take on the role of helper, caretaker or fixer.

2 **You tend to jump into situations to help**

    You don't think twice: where help is needed, you're there! You might unconsciously be scanning the environment or the situation for where help will be needed so that you can get in there first.

3 **You anticipate people's needs before they do**

    You might know what's needed in a situation before anyone else does or even know what a person needs even if they're not aware of it. You may get bored or anxious if there isn't a problem to solve or someone to help!

4 **You experience helper's high**

You get good feelings – a rush of endorphins – when you help or fix something. There's nothing wrong with this of course, as long as it isn't a compulsion.

5 **You like being independent**

You like to figure things out on your own and feel you can figure things out yourself with enough time and effort.

6 **You may feel that you don't deserve help**

You may believe that you're fine and that your needs and your work aren't that big a deal, so why should anybody support or help you? What you're doing is just what's expected. It's the bare minimum. You might walk around with a belief that: 'doesn't everyone do this?' Notice that this is suspiciously similar to imposter phenomenon thinking.

7 **You can have outbursts of anger and not understand why**

You might give so much that you start to feel drained. But you don't pull back or look after yourself. You don't acknowledge the fact that you might need some space, and feelings of guilt arise at the thought of doing so. So your frustration comes out in an outburst of anger.

8 **You can get annoyed with other people who do ask for help**

People who ask for what they need might annoy you. It may look like they're making a fuss for nothing and you perceive them as complainers or as being unnecessarily weak and holding everyone back.

9 **You have problems articulating your own feelings and needs**

Even if you were OK with asking for help, you wouldn't really know how to because you're not used to doing it. You might not even be sure what a feeling or need is!

10 **You're uncomfortable being vulnerable**

This is the underlying factor beneath these patterns of thinking and behaving: a discomfort with feeling vulnerable and uncertain. Where some might default to aggression/blaming or checking out and ignoring their deeper need for reassurance, you jump in and rescue. It's a habitual, survival mechanism to defend against uncertainty.

Of course, none of these behaviours is inherently problematic. The quality of caring is a beautiful one. It's when the behaviours are compulsive and out of step with what's really needed in a situation that problems arise. Awareness is the first step to using your capacities with moderation and wisdom so that you are making your best contribution (not just a habitual, compulsive one informed by external pressures and expectations).

SELF-REFLECTION   Rescuing behaviours

How many of these rescuer patterns do you experience?

What's the advantage of each?

What's the disadvantage?

Who would you be without them?

Toxic work myths

Where do these trapping identities come from? Of course, childhood experiences, schooling and the culture we grew up in have a strong role. But this book won't focus on these early life experiences. We've discussed the wider, global and Western societal context in the previous chapters; here we'll continue examining the organizational context and the work culture myths (sometimes confused with 'work ethic') that we can get caught up in. Earlier we looked at identities that trap; now let's look at complementary work myths that trap and how they interact with the identities that trap.

The myth of productivity

We've touched on how our current version of capitalism and shareholder value maximization business strategy can lead to overloading and overworking the workforce. As a result, people believe they have to be constantly productive and busy or risk losing their jobs. In fact, what we've seen in the past few decades is that putting people under pressure to create outputs and profit can have catastrophic effects of global proportions. The 2008 global recession is an example.

'Do more with less' is a mantra that has taken root as companies have sought to make efficiency gains post-recession. As workloads continue to increase and become more complex in the VUCA world, an obsession has developed with productivity tools and time management hacks. But economic data, in the United States for example, saw that productivity (measured as the amount of goods and services produced with the number of hours or work to produce them) is only increasing by 1.4 per cent per year, the lowest growth rate in 30 years (Sprague, 2017). It turns out that a 'do more, faster' mindset isn't actually how people want to work, and that 61 per cent say they want to 'slow down to get things right' (Taylor, 2019).

From a physical perspective, it's easier to notice when the body has reached its limits, but in a knowledge economy, it's harder for people to notice when their judgement is impaired until it's too late. For example, medical errors cost people lives. The US Agency for Healthcare Research and Quality has recognized that fatigue is characterized as a latent hazard and 'an unsafe condition' in health care (AHRQ, 2019). However, interventions to improve patient safety by ensuring doctors and other health professionals have enough rest and recovery time are still in their infancy. While the research into which tasks are most affected by which type of fatigue is also limited, we know that if we're constantly overwhelmed and under pressure, our survival (fight/flight) mechanism kicks in and our higher level thinking is switched off to preserve energy and focus on immediate threats (AHRQ, 2019).

In a way, the fact that tasks can be automated and mechanized is potentially a good thing for people's health and happiness – provided we can get through the transition without sacrificing the current workforce's ability to make a living. In the long term, a larger proportion of repetitive work could be done by machines, while humans do the more creative and relational work. In the next chapter we'll explore what it looks like to work using a Creative Cycles model that taps into our higher cognitive faculties, rather than a mechanical productivity model that relies on physical work or repetitive cognitive tasks.

The myth of meritocracy

One of the first courses at Harvard University to be provided as an online version was called *Justice* and was run by Harvard philosophy professor Michael Sandel (Sandel, 2020). I took the online course myself as a doctoral student and remember how much it resonated with me. It helped to start liberating me from the weight of external expectations as I understood the origins of my academic and professional success in a wider context. Awareness is the beginning of transformation!

Within the lecture halls of one of the world's most elite universities, he challenges students to rethink their ideas of meritocracy, through the lens of their own achievement of getting into Harvard. He remarks that true meritocracy is an impossible system. It may well be preferable to nepotism or other systems for distributing position and power in an arbitrary way that is not based on talent and ability. But he demonstrates that an individual's progress in a meritocracy is based on those talents and abilities that one *happens to have*; conditions of birth (most people in his lecture were first-borns); and upbringing and education that are *not of one's own making*. Therefore, no one can truly say that their success is merited on the basis of their own efforts (Sandel, 2020). While this may seem confronting at first, it provides a way out of the Success Trap by acknowledging that we are not fully in control of our success. Your life outcomes – including your successes – are predetermined to a significant extent, which should take a weight off your shoulders! This doesn't mean you should cave in to imposter-type thoughts. It should simply help balance out the weight of responsibility you feel in succeeding against the fact that you're partly the product of causes that came before you were born.

Now let's look at some key findings on how children are taught about effort and success. A study of 400 children in a US public school by Professor Carol Dweck examined the effects of praise. As a result of the study, parents the world over switched their parenting style and started praising their children for effort rather than results (or factors outside their children's control like intelligence) (Dweck, 1999).

For example, instead of saying, 'Well done on getting an A in your exam' they'll say, 'Well done on working hard on your exam.' In addition, the findings indicated that children praised for results (factors outside their control) rather than for effort (factors within their control) tended to choose easier puzzles rather than challenging ones when given a choice. Those praised for effort also bounced back after a failure and did much better whereas those praised for results or intelligence did worse on a follow-up test. Unsurprisingly, failure affected the kids praised for results and intelligence worse than the others. Strikingly, the brightest girls were affected the most by these effects and tended to collapse the worst after a failure, if praised for success rather than effort.

In the study summary, the lead concluded that, 'When we praise children for their intelligence, we tell them that this is the name of the game: look smart, don't risk making mistakes' (Bronson, 2007). What does this tell us? Perhaps the message is this: believing that you must live up to a certain standard, and to external expectations, reduces your willingness to experiment and learn from failure. In other words, it damages your resilience and gets in the way of creativity and expressing your full potential.

The myth of success as an organizing principle for life

The modern professional high achiever is someone who wields exceptional analytical abilities and specialized knowledge. They're usually someone who did well academically – but not necessarily. They almost certainly have a cluster of patterns of thought, feeling and behaviour where *success is an organizing principle*.

What's wrong with that? As discussed so far in this book, the Success Trap is a career or life situation that is pretty much a survival strategy. It has enabled you to succeed according to external expectations that aren't necessarily aligned with your deeper potential, values and aspirations. It's also a set of habits of thinking and behaving that get in the way of further growth and risk-taking needed for the next phase of your career and life.

The High Achiever Paradox then kicks in as a double-bind: past successes start to diminish the capacity for risk-taking, imagination and creativity, in order to protect current successes. This dilemma is particularly acute for high achievers in the knowledge economy, as the logical and analytical hard skills (so-called left brain functions) that made them successful are in diametrical opposition to the risk-taking, imaginative and collaborative soft skills (so-called right brain functions) that are needed to experiment with new ideas, pathways and even relationships. At the core is a fear of vulnerability.

This leads to the experience of 'despair despite success'. Existentialist psychiatrist Viktor Frankl reflects on a study where Harvard University graduates were surveyed after 20 years, noting that (externally validated) success didn't correlate directly with life satisfaction (Frankl, 1988). These were lawyers and doctors who had success in their professional as well as marital lives. But they complained that their lives 'were pointless and meaningless'. Existentialists would claim that to reach success in the form validated by society is not a sufficient condition for reaching a healthy purpose in life. To conform to society's norms without investing our full potential and abilities into our endeavours will bring despair. Conversely, if we're able to discover a vocation that is particularly well suited and fitting, we will experience fulfilment. We'll come back to the vocational life (in contrast to work-life balance) in Chapter 10.

THE HIGH ACHIEVER'S SECRET DREAM

So what do you choose as a career when the best part of a million dollars has been invested in your education? Despite having spent 24 years of my life in education, in some of the most elite institutions in the world, I felt it wasn't enough. By the time I'd jumped through a multitude of professional hoops including a Master's, a PhD and several other professional qualifications, I was confused. Why did the goalposts keep moving? Surely it wasn't this hard to help people, which is why I went into medicine, research and population health in the first place?

Eventually, it dawned on me: *the goalposts would never stop moving*. It's just how the system worked. That's when I made a decision to stop jumping and trust that life would show me where to go next. My reality filter changed – I was seeing more clearly – and so my decisions seemed counter-intuitive. After all, what I'd always wanted was a sense of fulfilment, but I needed to drop the need for validation and achievement first. I also needed to let go of the need for certainty and be willing to take more risks, which was a turning point as mentioned before. That's when things fell into place. Opportunities came my way and I was able to do work I really loved with the United Nations for a period of time. Eventually, I found my way to independence through setting up my own business in Transformational Coaching and Consulting.

Learning from the High Achiever Paradox

The high achiever's experience can illuminate the cost of succeeding on the outside and feeling trapped on the inside. It is a cultural phenomenon that needs to evolve if we're to harness the best of our human abilities in service to something beyond our fears and basic needs. We're at risk of burnout, especially if we buy into the myth of meritocracy and believe our success is all of our own making, or if we fail to understand the mental mechanics of imposterism. We face the dilemma of succeeding on the hamster wheel of life at the expense of a sense of peace, happiness and fulfilment – particularly on a deeper level. Some of the paradoxes we've uncovered in this chapter are:

- the need for validation and significance while dismissing praise;
- the need for the next challenge despite feeling tired or overwhelmed;
- the need for more qualifications/credentials/training despite having plenty;
- the fear of failure despite a track record of success;
- happiness not because of success but despite it.

The only way I know to resolve the High Achiever Paradox is to develop awareness around the thinking patterns and behaviours that construct it and then to transform the underlying assumptions. Similarly, to break out of an identity that holds us back (including one that is reinforced by the environment), we have to investigate the beliefs and assumptions that created it. It's not always easy – and you may cringe when you see the effect of some of your patterns more clearly – but it's the most worthwhile work I know.

SHIFTING PERSPECTIVE: THE PATH OF THE RECOVERING OVERACHIEVER

There's nothing like a brush with death to put things into perspective. But there's no need to go to those lengths. Bronnie Ware, a palliative care nurse who looked after people with terminal illnesses, documented the regrets that people faced as they were preparing for the end (Steiner, 2012):

1 I wish I'd had the courage to live a life true to myself, not the life others expected of me.
2 I wish I hadn't worked so hard.
3 I wish I'd had the courage to express my feelings.
4 I wish I'd stayed in touch with my friends.
5 I wish I'd let myself be happier.

Note that none of them included: 'I wish I'd worked harder' or 'I wish I was more successful'.

Just like when you go to the doctor, once the root cause of the problem is accurately diagnosed, an intervention is more effective. Otherwise, treatment will be largely symptomatic or even make things worse. You realize how you've been holding yourself back and start to refuse to continue sacrificing who you really are on the altar of who you think you should be. Fortunately, transformational wisdom and methodologies like mindfulness and coaching are becoming increasingly mainstream, and there appears to be growing awareness in organizations of the importance of staff wellbeing and sustainability. It is beginning to translate into some changes in how companies operate. An example is the work on psychological safety (Edmonson, 2018), which we'll return to in Part Three.

For us as individuals and from a humanistic perspective, the good life is not the same as achievement (Winston, 2015). The good life is a process, not a fixed state or place to get to.

Now you've got a solid grounding in the context and identities to be aware of, let's get into the transformational work.

PART TWO

Breaking free from the Success Trap

CHAPTER FOUR

Goal-driven versus creative flow

So now that you know what the Success Trap is, and the various ways it can express itself in people's lives and careers, how do you break free of this trap? In this chapter, we'll look at the alternative to the goal-driven, 'Success Trap' life. We'll explore the idea of creativity – not as an artistic activity, but as a way of living and engaging with the world.

Creativity may give you an advantage in the workplace. As of 2020, a large survey of 660 million professional profiles found that creativity was the number one soft skill companies seemed to be hiring for (Sevilla, 2020). Creativity is also prized by organizational leaders. IBM, a company that has successfully reinvented itself despite fierce competition from Apple, refers to creativity as the reason why agile companies create and sustain a high return on investment (ROI). Its global survey of 1,500 CEOs (IBM, 2010) found that leaders deemed creativity to be the most important quality for leadership.

The prison of the goal-driven life

I always think it's somewhat tragic that while we live in an essentially goal-driven culture, psychologists know full well that we humans are pretty bad at predicting what will make us happy (Gilbert, 2006). Even if we do experience a sense of accomplishment from reaching a goal, it never lasts for long. It's the anti-climax of finishing a big project or finally getting married: you're delighted for a period of time, but quickly default back to the goal-chasing state. What's the *next* big project; the *next* step in your relationship? With a goal-driven life, we can easily live in a perpetual gap between where we are and where we want to get to, without ever permanently reaching the elusive happiness or success we're working towards.

The good thing about goals

I'm not arguing against having goals altogether. There's plenty of evidence that it's important to have goals and to take action towards them. Otherwise, the thing you're aiming for is just an idea, and no real progress can be made. Certainly, it makes sense to articulate goals, write them down, take action and be accountable to organize your energy and time. Being accountable to others is also a powerful catalyst. One study calculated how much more likely you are to achieve your goals based on how serious you are about them, by dividing participants into five groups:

- Group 1 was asked to simply think about the goals they hoped to accomplish within a four-week block.
- Groups 2 to 5 were asked to write down their goals.
- Group 3 was also asked to write action commitments for each goal.
- Group 4 had both to write goals and action commitments and also share these commitments with a friend.

- Group 5 went the furthest by doing all of the above plus sending a weekly progress report to a friend.

Those in Group 1 accomplished 43 per cent of their stated goals. Those in Group 4 accomplished 64 per cent of their stated goals, while those in Group 5 were the most successful, with an average 76 per cent of their goals accomplished (Gardner and Albee, 2013).

So, the evidence shows that having goals and taking action on them is useful. But we also know that becoming trapped in a cycle of endless goal-seeking is a significant element of the Success Trap – so when does working towards goals become unhealthy? The answer, like many things in life, is when it becomes a *compulsion* rather than a choice. When you're unable to sit still for a moment and just breathe; when you have to be doing something all the time and your attention has to be occupied constantly; when it leads to exhaustion and costs you your health and relationships. We could call this phenomenon 'goal addiction'.

Overcoming goal addiction

Any addiction – from chocolate and cigarettes, to work and the office – involves the reward centres of the brain. These are the parts of the brain that tell you what you should chase, and give you a hit of pleasurable dopamine when you get it. Every time you get a dopamine hit for achieving a goal, your brain remembers what you did to achieve that goal – it learns. Soon it doesn't care what you have to do to achieve the goal, you just know you want to achieve it. While there isn't a huge amount of research on processes such as goal-setting or goal achievement, it stands to reason that if you feel good about yourself for setting and achieving goals, it's something you'll want to keep doing. Again, it's not that goal-setting is a problem in itself, it's when it becomes a compulsive way of behaving at the cost of your health and sanity (ie an addiction) that it can become a problem.

Life and business coach Tony Robbins talks about how addictions are bad strategies for meeting our human needs (Robbins, 2014). If a pattern of thought or behaviour – like goal-setting – meets three or more of your needs, you become addicted, and the behaviour becomes compulsive rather than a choice. The consequence is, of course, that you can burn out or waste your energy on meaningless goals that are not aligned with your deeper potential and values. Robbins, who builds on psychologist Abraham Maslow's theory of human needs and motivation (Maslow, 1943), explains that we have four basic human needs that must be fulfilled one way or another. These, he describes as survival needs of the personality (Table 4.1):

1 certainty/safety;
2 uncertainty/challenge;
3 significance;
4 connection.

In addition, there are two higher needs that are connected to our deeper potential rather than to survival:

5 learning/growth;
6 contribution.

While the first four can lead to a satisfactory life, it's the latter two that lead to fulfilment. According to Robbins, if a behaviour like goal-setting or goal achievement meets three or more of your six human needs, you may become addicted to goal-setting or goal achievement. As a high achiever, your ability to achieve goals successfully means you're likely to meet your need for challenge, significance, connection (for example, by working with teams) and safety (for example, your bosses will validate you and pay you for it). If you enjoy learning and making a difference, you'll also meet your need for growth and contribution. So, all your human needs can be satisfied because you're great at setting and achieving goals!

TABLE 4.1 Why goal-setting can be addictive

Type of need	Need	Underlying belief/strategy to meet the need
Basic (survival) need	Safety	Working towards goals helps me create security for myself and my family
	Uncertainty	Going for my goals keeps me moving and my life interesting; I never get bored
	Significance	Achieving goals gives me a sense of accomplishment and respect from others
	Connection	Working on goals with others gives me a sense of connection
Higher (fulfilment) need	Learning/ growth	I learn new skills as I work towards my goals
	Contribution	As I set meaningful goals with social value, I help others

CASE STUDY John

Becoming aware of how you're using goal-setting as a strategy to meet your needs enables you to make more informed and deliberate choices. You may even find healthier and more diverse ways to meet your needs.

John is an executive in a global bank. His two most important needs are significance and connection. He tries to meet his need for significance by working extremely hard, which drives him to work long hours and skip family commitments. He's very effective at setting financial targets and meeting them for his organization and his family. He tries to meet his need for connection by sharing any struggles with his family – he talks about himself, and his work, and how stressful it is. He misses their school events and his wife complains that he doesn't spend enough time with her. He emphasizes what a responsibility it is and that he is doing it for them. Over the years, he finds that his children don't feel so connected to him and that his wife has grown distant.

He feels he's got significance at work but is losing connection with his family. What can he do?

One possibility for John, once he becomes aware of how he is using work and goal-setting to meet his personality needs, is to focus on developing a better connection strategy. The little time he spends with his family could be devoted to listening to his wife and children and supporting them in any way he can rather than talking about his own struggles or trying to fix problems rather than listen deeply. He could strengthen and diversify his support system to include a leadership group or executive coach rather than relying on offloading to his family. This would enable him to reflect on the challenges he's facing at work and resolve them constructively instead of simply venting. He may also need to manage his commitments better by asking whether his priorities are aligned with his deeper values. A well-timed reflection and change of behaviour could save his marriage and family life while supporting his career.

SWAPPING BEHAVIOURS

One way to overcome addiction is by substituting one strategy for a healthier one that is more aligned with what you care deeply about – swapping an unhelpful or unhealthy behaviour for a healthier one. For example, an unhealthy strategy for meeting a need for safety might be compulsive goal-setting behaviour that is informed by a belief such as, 'if I meet this next financial goal, I will feel my family is safe'. A more helpful and sustainable strategy for meeting the same need for safety might be to have a meaningful conversation with your family about what helps them feel safe and review expenses. You may be surprised by what you find and feel a weight lift from your shoulders. You'll probably be reminded of what really matters in relationships and that you've always found a way to look after yourself and your family before.

Now try for yourself (use the layout in Table 4.2). What are your top two needs in life? Note that the ranking can change over time:

1 certainty/safety;

2 uncertainty/challenge;

3 significance/respect;

4 connection;

5 learning/growth;

6 contribution.

What is one way you meet each need?

TABLE 4.2   Meeting needs

Certainty/safety	How do I meet this need in my life?
Certainty/safety	
Uncertainty/challenge	
Significance/respect	
Connection	
Learning/growth	
Contribution	

Now think of a behaviour you would like to change. How many needs does it help you meet? How else could you meet these needs that might be healthier, more aligned and perhaps even more fun?

Goal-setting fatigue and recovery

'I'm so glad you're not getting me to do that goal-setting stuff,' a doctor emphatically declared after an initial coaching conversation. Like many high achievers she knows how to make things happen. High achievers are often the person who can see what's needed and they're ready to do what it takes. This usually makes them very valuable to their teams and organizations. But as we've seen, it can also lead to getting caught in the Success Trap, and consequently, to burnout and fatigue. The underlying expectation for many high achievers is that they should always know their goals and purpose/vision, and that *not* knowing these means something is wrong and they need to figure it out and start setting some new goals. But this is not necessarily the case.

High achievers can underestimate how much time, energy and cognitive effort they are consuming as they go about their daily lives. They tend to take success for granted and see failure as an aberration (rather than as something normal in a human life). This isn't helped by a culture of go-getting and success chasing where we will often be exposed to other people's successes, but not the journey and invisible trials and tribulations that led them there, including the 'failures' necessary for the learning process. So the first thing in recovering from goal-setting fatigue is to be aware of what achieving a goal truly requires.

The truth is that achieving something requires many components including focus, failure and a bit of luck. The Navy SEALs go through some of the toughest military training in the world. They are very familiar with what it takes to achieve a goal. Here are the SEALs' principles for success (Murphy, 2015):

1 Develop mental toughness.
2 Set (and achieve) micro-goals.
3 Visualize success and overcome failure.
4 Convince yourself you can do it.
5 Control your emotions.

So far, so good, right? But there is a sixth principle: *rest and recovery*. This is the space between goals, which people trapped in goal-driven behaviour can forget to allow for. Without this recovery time, you can never truly reach your potential since your mind doesn't have time to reflect, learn, integrate and prepare for the next cycle of activity. Notice that item (4) above can be addressed through self-enquiry and reflection, and that item (5) refers to self-regulation. We'll go into both of these in depth in Chapter 6.

If you have reached goal-setting fatigue and need some emergency help to slow down and take a step back before you burn out, go to Chapter 5. Otherwise, the box lists a few quick ideas for dealing with goal-setting fatigue.

DEALING WITH GOAL-SETTING FATIGUE: STARTER PACK

1 Have fewer goals

Warren Buffett's career advice to his pilot was to identify and focus on the top five goals that he wanted to achieve in his lifetime. Everything else below the top five went on an 'avoid at all costs' list (Oshin, nd).

2 Use micro-goals

You don't always have to have big goals. Navy SEALs get through Hell Week by chunking it into small steps: get through breakfast, get to the camp, do the push-ups, etc. (Clarine, nd; Navy SEALs, nd).

3 Focus on experiences rather than things

Experiences include learning, contribution, connection. Favour these over things like a job or a romantic partner; this means you can create the experience any time with the opportunities you have around you.

4 Get comfortable with the unknown

Meaningful change requires stepping into uncertain territory and making friends with the discomfort of the unknown (especially if you're used to being in control!).

From rigid goal-setter to creator in flow

As we have seen, one way to break an addiction or get rid of an unhealthy, unhelpful behaviour is to replace it with a healthier, more helpful behaviour. I should emphasize that the most important aspect of replacing the behaviour is bringing awareness to the behaviours and the thoughts and feelings associated with them, which we'll explore in Chapter 6. Here we're looking at what kind of possibilities are available to you for new behaviours as a by-product of expanding your awareness and committing to change. So once we have escaped from the trap of goal addiction and given ourselves a break from goal fatigue, what can we replace it with? I believe that the opposite of being goal-driven is not being goal-less; it is being in *creative flow*.

Flow

You may recognize flow as a state of mind colloquially known as 'being in the zone'. It's what happens when the High Achiever Paradox is resolved and there is a balance between focus and flexibility. The term comes from psychologist Mihaly Csikszentmihályi, in his seminal work *Flow: The psychology of optimal experience* (Csikszentmihályi, 1990). He observed that people are happiest when they are in a state of flow, which he described as a state of concentration or complete absorption with an activity that they're engaged in *for its own sake*. This is a key difference between being goal-driven and being in a state of flow; a goal-driven task is done for the sake of the goal, whereas entering a state of flow is about the activity for the activity's sake.

You may have experienced a flow state and noticed that time flies, basic needs like food are ignored and every action, movement and thought unfolds perfectly from the previous one. You're *in the zone*. Csikszentmihályi characterized nine component states of achieving flow: 1) balance between the level of challenge and level of skill; 2) merging of action and awareness (your ego or perception of 'a "me" doing something' is switched off); 3) clarity of goals in the moment (clarity of motivation, prioritization, small steps, absence of inner conflict); 4) immediate and unambiguous feedback; 5) concentration on the task at hand; 6) paradox of control (relinquishing control leads to greater control); 7) transformation of time (it flies by); 8) loss of self-consciousness; and 9) autotelic experience (experience for its own sake) (Fullagar and Kelloway, 2009).

You can shift from goal-setter to creator by simply shifting your attitude to outcomes. Rather than setting fixed goals and working towards them, you can articulate possibilities and uncover creative solutions to the obstacles that come up. Rather than making something happen, you're removing the obstacles so that the actions unfold effortlessly.

Artist and sculptor Michelangelo is believed to have said:

The sculpture is already complete within the marble block, before I start my work. It is already there, I just have to chisel away the superfluous material... Every block of stone has a statue inside it and it is the task of the sculptor to discover it. I saw the angel in the marble and carved until I set him free.

In other words, your environment isn't there to be used for your goals. Instead, you can acknowledge that you're engaged in an interactive process between your environment and your creative inspiration – like a conversation. You're engaging with life more like an artist than a mechanic.

But why aren't we more connected to this creative way of engaging with life? Why is pushing to achieve goals still the dominant cultural model of productivity?

What is creativity?

Many definitions of creativity exist. Most of us are familiar with the idea that creativity extends beyond art forms like painting or writing, but it can be difficult to pin down what it actually *is*. In a 2016 US study of creativity, it was defined as 'the ability to come up with original ideas, think in a detailed and elaborative way, synthesize information, and be open-minded and curious' (Kim, 2016). Ok then, that's all well and good... but what does it mean for your life? How can you recognize it and cultivate it?

General traits among people considered creative in the wider sense were identified in the 2016 study. These include:

- **Big-picture-thinking**: thinking abstractly, looking past the concrete details of the current situation and seeking new solutions. This optimism and curiosity are sometimes seen as dreamy and unrealistic.
- **Spontaneity**: a tendency to be flexible and act fast on new opportunities, approaching them with an open mind and a playful perspective, which can come off as impulsive.
- **Playfulness**: light-heartedness and a drive to explore the world, which can be perceived as mischievous.
- **Resilience**: picking yourself up after a failure and bouncing back from challenges, refocusing on new ways to overcome adversities. Sometimes, this comes across as combative.
- **Autonomy**: striving for independence in your thoughts and actions, relying on intrinsic motivation to pursue goals. At times, such individuals can seem out of control.
- **Defiance**: a tendency to reject existing norms and authorities in pursuit of their own ideas. This allows you to see what others cannot see and develop solutions that push boundaries, which can seem rebellious.

- **Risk-taking**: fuelled by their optimism, many creative people are willing to forgo security in favour of uncertain rewards. To the average person, this may come across as reckless.
- **Daydreaming**: by daydreaming, creative individuals are able to envision new perspectives and solutions – but along the way, some of their ideas might seem delusional.

As you can see, these traits are not specific to a cultural stereotype of the 'creative'. They reflect the wider creative ability that we all have in facing life and its challenges. Here's a simple definition of creativity, then, for the purposes of this book: *creativity is the ability to combine previously existing elements in a new way*. No paint or musical instruments needed. Just a functioning imagination!

CREATIVE CYCLES

One thing scientists seem to agree on is that creativity is a process rather than a personality and that a brilliant idea, or solution to your problem, usually comes after a period of incubation (Ritter and Dijksterhuis, 2014). This seems to have four stages:

- preparation (acquisition of knowledge on some task);
- incubation (process that occurs when conscious attention is diverted away from the task);
- illumination (creative idea flashes into sight);
- verification (creative idea is subjected to evaluation). (Wallas, 1926)

In other words, the brilliant idea, which might be an insight about your next step regarding a dream job or your big mission in life, comes after you've gathered information and then taken your focus *off* trying to find the answer (Ritter and Dijksterhuis, 2014).

As you can intuit, this process requires you to be ok with 'not knowing' for a while as you sit in the incubation period where the elements you've gathered are recombining with knowledge and

---

experience already stored in your subconscious. Because the incubation period of creativity requires slowing down external activities, it can fly in the face of a modern culture where you need to be constantly doing something. We have to make a conscious effort to create some peace and quiet.

'Aha' moments are associated with alpha waves and occur when we are less active mentally and physically. Alpha brainwaves are slower and higher in amplitude than beta waves, which occur when we are fully alert and engaged in routine activities and conversations. You experience alpha waves when you sit down to rest, take time out to reflect or meditate (Scientific American, 1997). Deadlines and trying to push through to get things done can be detrimental to your inner genius, whereas rest, exercise and daydreaming will help generate ideas.

Creative flow in practice

In 1661, the son of a farmer was admitted to Cambridge University to study. An outbreak of the Black Death forced him to return home until it abated. One day, while spending time in an orchard, he noticed an apple fall to the ground and wondered why it fell in a straight line. At that moment, not in a library, not in a lecture theatre, and certainly not in front of a computer, Isaac Newton had an insight that led to an idea. It hatched a whole new system of thought and transformed our understanding of the physical world – gravity.

While we don't understand the full social psychology explaining the origins of great ideas, many such anecdotes of inspired insights exist. Newton is one famous example. Others include Archimedes' *eureka* moment in the bath. Albert Einstein wrote his most famous papers on the theory of relativity outside the confines of academia. He wasn't deemed good enough for an academic post at the time and worked as a clerk in a patent office. He was turned down for a promotion because his bosses thought he didn't understand technology well enough! Beatle Paul McCartney came up with the famous song *Let it Be* after dreaming that his mother, who had died from cancer when he was 14, visited him and reassured him that, '*It's gonna be OK. Just let it be...*' (McCartney, 2019). It's a recurring theme: the best ideas seem to come up at unexpected times or in unusual situations when you're not hyper-focused on getting things done or solving a problem.

You've probably had the experience yourself of having a problem that you'd spent some time trying to figure out to no avail, only for the solution to come to you as an 'aha moment' when you were doing something completely different. You may not think of yourself as a 'creative person', but in that moment, you were being creative, just like Newton, Archimedes, Einstein and McCartney. The psychological process was the same.

So how can we develop this creativity and access the ability more purposefully? The key ingredient is worrying less about what others think of you, switching off your inner critic and letting go of self-anxiety (Jacobs, 2017). If you're harsh and critical with yourself as you try to come up with a solution, your creativity will be dampened. But flow goes beyond the problem of the harsh inner critic. It requires that we completely forget ourselves in the first place and make way for pure creative thinking. Can you imagine what it would be like if your concerns about safety and survival evaporated and you lived in flow?

Here are two key principles, validated neuroscientifically, from ancient wisdom traditions like mindfulness.

LET GO OF WHAT PEOPLE THINK OF YOU (SWITCH OFF YOUR SOCIAL SELF)
It's almost impossible for human beings not to care what others think. We're social animals and have a biological need for belonging and connection, so we develop ways of behaving that fit in – this helps us feel safe and connected. The downside is that this need for belonging and ability to act socially can suppress our independent thinking and creative ideation. What happens if we switch off this instinct for monitoring other people's opinions?

Eadweard Muybridge moved from the UK to the United States and set up a successful antique book shop. However, he had a serious road accident and a severe head injury to the front of his brain that left him with double vision, confused thinking and an impaired sense of taste and smell. But he also developed eccentric behaviour – the social inhibition instinct in his brain appeared to have been damaged and seemed not to work anymore. He stopped caring what people thought! Following this injury, his career path transformed and he became a world-famous photographer and pioneer in photography and motion pictures.

It's thought that the injury to the part of the brain responsible for social inhibition unleashed Muybridge's creativity (Shimamura, 2002). Similar conclusions have been drawn from imaging the brains of masterful jazz musicians while they perform. MRI scans show that areas of the brain that monitor for social approval are switched off while they perform and that this leads to the emergence of spontaneous creative activity – the improvizational quality that is typical of jazz (Limb and Braun, 2008). Hopefully, you're not going to rely on a brain injury like Eadweard Muybridge to release any inhibitions about being more spontaneous and therefore more creative! Awareness is the key, as we'll continue to explore in Chapter 6.

LET GO OF WHAT YOU THINK OF YOU (SWITCH OFF YOUR NARRATIVE SELF)
We all have narratives about who we are and what we do in our lives and we love sharing them (Tamir and Mitchell, 2012). If repeated over time, these narratives become an identity. These can be social roles like daughter, doctor, wife, or archetypes like hero/rescuer, rebel, lover. However, the idea of a fixed 'you' is flawed. The self is constantly changing and with the growing understanding of the brain as neuroplastic, we know that learning and moulding of our patterns of thinking and behaving is a lifelong process if we so choose. So who are you really beyond the narratives associated with labels like daughter/son, sister, expert, partner, etc?

Who you think of as 'you' is in fact a series of interlinked processes and memories in your mind. So far, neuroscience has not been able to locate an isolated part of the brain where the personality is found. On the contrary, a network of connections linking different parts of the brain creates the experience of being 'me', the story of 'me' and the memories of 'me'.

What's interesting is that the absence of a coherent persona has been found to be a hallmark of creative genius. Creative geniuses are more likely to display contradictory behaviours and tendencies rather than one coherent personality (Csikszentmihályi, 2013). People we would categorize as geniuses in their levels of intelligence or quality of output appear to be more interested in the variety of thought processes and experiences available to them than fitting into a fixed personality or identity.

PRACTICE CREATIVITY: ARE YOU IN FEAR OR IN FLOW?

Here are a few suggestions for bringing more creativity into your life (whatever form it might take for you):

1 Mindset

   A creator is the opposite of a victim and sees a wider range of choice and possibility in everything. Carefully examine, address and weed out all excuses that come up as you try to take a creative step forward. Ask yourself: *am I in fear or in flow?*

2 Strategy

   Get involved in a creative activity every day, whether it's a hobby, or a more creative approach to work (see the creativity traits above). Identify what is repetitive in your work and whether to modify, cut, outsource or delegate it over a period of time.

3 Actions

Make time, however short, to be deliberately creative by putting a regular time slot in your calendar. Include: 1) quiet time (see Chapter 5 for ways to do this if your schedule is overwhelming); and 2) your creative endeavour of choice. Create accountability and reward. Find support if necessary.

Make space for creativity in your life and creativity will come. Every time something feels automatic review and evolve it. You'll feel more alive and you could also make your job more interesting as a result...

Creating a new career

Whether it is creating a painting, a job or a career, creating something long term is a marathon rather than a sprint. This can feel like a problem if a sudden change of circumstance has occurred unexpectedly – like a redundancy or illness – and your bank account is suffering. For some people, a mid-life career change might only involve a change of scenery without any deeper transformation. For others, though, it can involve a radical re-evaluation of who they want to be, the balance they want to experience and the values they want to live by. They're creating much more than a new job or career. They're experiencing a change of identity and letting go of patterns of thinking and acting that no longer serve them (Ibarra, 2003).

People undertaking this kind of reinvention go through six stages in a creative cycle. It's a cycle that allows space for incubation, learning and 'failing' as they take action.

Here are the six stages:

1 **Relax:** The world can be an overwhelming and confusing place. Take a step back and increase your self-care. The reduced cognitive load creates mental space and reduces brain

fog and reactivity. We'll go more deeply into this and ways to make space in your life in Chapter 5.

2 **Reflect:** Now that you have made space for your creative thinking, take time to sit with the big questions like 'what do you really want?' and 'who do you want to become as a person in this next phase of your career?' Notice the thoughts and assumptions that come up. This may stir up strong emotions of fear and excitement. This is where some of the deeper shifts in perspective occur as old, limiting beliefs and presuppositions are challenged. We'll discuss a specific process to do this (self-enquiry) in Chapter 6.

3 **Release:** As you allow for deeper enquiry of your thoughts, an insight is likely to occur. You'll hit upon something that may have been weighing you down or holding you back. This can be emotional. You may also feel a surge of energy that was trapped by a limiting belief. In Chapter 6 we'll look at ways to help you stay calm and clear as you go through the cycle of change.

4 **Reconnect:** As you break free of old expectations and patterns, new ideas and thoughts will emerge. The fog will dispel and your inner genius will spark new ideas. Practically, you may get clarity over which people, places and habits are right for you to align with. You'll connect with your deeper vision and values.

5 **Respond:** From this place you are well equipped for action. You may find yourself motivated or inspired to send an email, a CV or finally resign and move on. A flexible strategy implemented in small, consistent steps is best. We'll look at a few tools for capturing your new ideas and actions around your purpose and mission in Chapter 7.

6 **Receive:** This is the hardest one for high achievers, because it can be perceived as passivity. But it's not. Learn to be patient and trust the journey and celebrate your efforts.

Of course, deep work like this is easier said than done, and people can and do get stuck at various stages of the cycle (Table 4.3).

TABLE 4.3 Creative cycle

	Main action needed	What might keep you stuck
Relax	Radical declutter (of your mind and environment) and quiet time	Fear of boredom. Most people find it hard to relax and find they spin their wheels trying to keep going
Reflect	Powerful questions that challenge pre-existing assumptions. Learning from the past. Taking stock	Overanalysing. Answering intellectually rather than spontaneously from the heart
Release	Being with intense emotions and letting them complete their course (eg, grief over the loss of a job)	Resistance to experiencing feelings
Reconnect	Capturing new ideas, values, mission or purpose	Indecisiveness and trying to perfect a plan. Overwhelmed at the scale of the vision you've uncovered
Respond	Test new ideas. Take immediate action in small steps. Take a bold leap where needed	Fear of failure. Taking on too much
Receive	Patience, celebration, letting go of the outcome and its exact timing	Need to control outcome and timing

It's entirely possible to recreate your career once, if not two or three times in this day and age (Meister, 2012), and you don't have to go through the process alone. Mentors, guides and communities of support who are aligned with your values can make the process a whole lot easier although you still have to do your own work and be grounded in yourself.

MICRO-CYCLES AND MACRO-CYCLES

The length of time of a single creative cycle varies enormously. A great idea can unfold over the span of a few moments, or an entire lifetime. Of course, within each larger (macro) cycle, there are smaller (micro) cycles. In 'goal speak' we might talk of smaller projects within larger projects. Unlike goals, however, the creative cycle is not about achieving something external. It's about expressing something internal – an idea, a vision, a mission – and intuiting the next action without forcing it.

CREATIVITY BOOSTERS AND KILLERS

You've probably noticed that there are times, places, people and habits who help you think outside the box and feel open to new ideas and possibilities. There may also be times, places, people and habits that dampen that quality of openness to new ideas in you.

For example, creativity boosters might include daydreaming, nature, being in the shower, being on holiday, listening to music (these activate alpha waves that are associated with creativity). Creativity killers might include stressful deadlines, highly critical or negative people, a lack of sleep or alcohol excess.

What helps you come up with great ideas? What are the times, people, places and habits that support or dampen your ability to come up with creative solutions?

The bottom line: you're not a machine

Many of us grew up in a culture in which creativity was under-valued – it doesn't seem like a path to a stable job and happy life. Productivity has become equated with automation and efficiency rather than innovation and spontaneity. Our brain has been moulded to serve the needs of an industrial knowledge economy that supports mass production, much of it to do with processing information and logical problem solving.

But humans need time and space to think their best thoughts. It's usually during rest, play or time in nature that the genius idea comes through; not while you're hyper-focused on information gathering or problem solving. I believe solving complex 21st-century problems requires that we drop the biggest productivity myth of all: that machine-like productivity is more valuable than genius-like creativity. Humans are still capable of being more innovative, adaptable, empathic and entrepreneurial than machines, which means there can be rich rewards for those who give space to their spontaneous creative ideation.

Next, we'll explore how to slow down and create space even if you have a busy life and big responsibilities.

CHAPTER FIVE

Slow down to speed up

It's difficult to create a new career and life if you're over-whelmed. In this chapter we'll look at the first part of the creative cycle – relaxing. Slowing down to speed up is a principle I learned when I started out in business: it helped me make decisions outside my habitual patterns of thinking and behaving.

CASE STUDY   Dea

When Dea contacted me, she had recently taken a career leap but felt she might be at risk of burnout. An award-winning marketing specialist in the pharmaceutical industry, she had just resigned from her demanding job. She wanted to dedicate more time to work she felt more aligned with, and to have more balance. Financial concerns were less prominent at this stage in her career, and she wanted to return to growing her holistic health practice. But she was in the habit of always being on the go, moving from one project to the next and putting others first.

One thing was clear to me: she needed a good dose of self-care. She also needed some space to grieve the end of an era. But Dea held a belief that she had to keep going. She believed that she mustn't let other people down and that she had to respond instantaneously to demands. Digging deeper into the beliefs around over-giving and doing too much at the expense of her own health and wellbeing, we found that she was holding onto a singular, damaging idea fuelling her stress: *it's ok for me to do things that are not ok with me.*

As we explored this over two or three months, she started to trust that it was ok for her not to respond to requests immediately, and even say 'no' to requests that she couldn't or didn't want to fulfil. The freedom and joy she felt made a difference to how she was showing up in meetings and relationships. After a few restorative weeks, she had a lot more energy – and was offered a part-time consulting role in a highly supportive firm, which allowed her to have an income doing work she enjoyed, while also having space to grow her holistic health practice and enjoy retreats in the wilderness with her community of practitioners.

The toxicity of constant urgency

Most people are unaware of how fast they are going in their life. What people often notice is the impact of it: stress, overwhelm, arguments, poor health, etc. Before they know it, another month, year or decade has gone by. If they do wake up to the fact that they're going too fast for their own good, they don't necessarily believe they can do much about it. But first, how do you know you're going too fast? You might have:

- an overwhelmed mind: thoughts out of control, preoccupied with anxiety about the future, regrets over the past;
- an overwhelmed body: tension, fatigue, can't relax, can't sleep, health problems.

You may also notice that you show up late; you make excuses you don't really believe; your kids and loved ones are constantly disappointed. Most importantly, you cut down on self-care and try to get more done in a frenzy.

What does being overwhelmed do to you?

- It kills your creativity – goodbye bright ideas and resilience.
- It stops you from enjoying the moment and what you already have.

The solution? It's time to slow down and make space. This may feel a bit counter-intuitive, as your instinct is to keep running on the treadmill. But you know deep down that you're going nowhere.

If you feel that your energy is scattered or spread too thin, it's likely that your focus is divided; you have too many demands pulling you in different directions. If you are not careful, this will lead to exhaustion and burnout. In this fast-paced, urgent, VUCA world, giving yourself permission to slow down is probably the kindest and wisest thing you'll ever do for yourself. Running around in a frenzy trying to get things done is often an attempt to keep things under control. We fear that if we stop for a moment, things will come crashing down. Many of us live like this every day, believing one or more of these thoughts:

- I don't have time for myself.
- If I'm not stressed, how will I get things done?
- I can't let people down.
- If I stop, something will go wrong.
- If I stop, I'll waste time.
- I don't want to be lazy.
- Etc.

The problem is that going too fast is counter-productive. First, the quality of your thinking is lower. Second, your energy reserves aren't replenished properly. A sense of urgency can set in and a vicious cycle is created. The faster you go, the more overwhelmed you feel; the more overwhelmed you feel, the faster you go... until a crisis happens.

THE BENEFITS OF A SLOW CULTURE

A survey of 1,500 leaders showed that rising complexity in a fast world was their top problem. A deeper understanding of issues, disinvesting from outdated modes of business and thinking more creatively were their favoured solutions (IBM, 2010). Some organizations appear to be recognizing that to stop firefighting and operate more sustainably, it is best to slow down (McGuire and Tang, 2011). In working with top teams, leaders at McKinsey & Co. found that not only was going fast not the answer to more productivity, but going fast made things more complex, consumed more energy and, in the best-case scenario, only partially solved some of the problems faced by the team. They found that when top teams slowed down, they were able to dig deeper into the challenges they faced and reached their objectives more quickly. They dealt more effectively with increased complexity and obstacles and they used less energy (Chang and Groeneveld, 2018).

How to create space

In the previous chapter, we looked at flowing with creative cycles rather than pushing to achieve goals. The first stage of the creative cycle was to *relax* – so let's looks at some practical ways to do just that.

HALT and up your self-care

When you're overwhelmed and busy, self-care is often the first thing to go. You're focused on getting things done and making sure everyone is taken care of while your diet, exercise and sleep take second place. But as we saw in Chapter 3, in an emergency situation on a flight, you're advised to put your oxygen mask on first before you help someone else. You're no use to anyone if you can't think properly from hypoxia. It's unfortunate that most people wait for a crisis or burnout before paying attention to their self-care (MacKian, 2002).The healthier approach to being overwhelmed is to increase your self-care, not sacrifice it. Optimal performance and self-care go hand in hand – ask any top-performing athlete or singer.

The basic things that keep you healthy are sleep, good diet and exercise. One of the most powerful tools to start cutting through the feeling of being overwhelmed is the acronym HALT: are you Hungry, Angry, Lonely or Tired? It's a tool for self-care and self-awareness to ensure you're not making decisions from a state of clouded judgement (Zomerland, 2014).

Make friends with time

Have you noticed how time can seem to fly by when you're having fun, or be really slow when you're bored? What we're thinking and feeling in any moment changes our experience – even our perception of time. Psychological time is what we enter when our mind revisits past memories or starts thinking about the future (Tolle, 2019). If you get caught up in regrets over the past or constant anxiety about the future, you're stuck in psychological time, as opposed to physical or 'real' time measured by a clock – since the moments you're thinking about are either gone or not here yet.

The best way to make friends with time is to be in the present moment, noticing if your mind jumps into the past or present and disconnects you from real time. This is at the heart of mindfulness. As the saying in the Zen tradition goes: *if not now, when?* By paying attention to what is in the present (rather than getting lost in proliferations of thought about the past or future), you are dealing with reality (not your anxiety about it). From here, it's easier for your mind to help you and come up with sensible ideas to deal with whatever is relevant in the moment. If you understand this principle, you may start to experience flow and get more done with less effort.

More done in less time?

In 2018, a financial services company embarked on a trial of a four-day working week while maintaining the same pay for its employees (FourDayWeek, 2020). It collaborated with researchers to examine the impact and reported that staff experienced more work-life balance and less stress. Microsoft tested the initiative in its Japan offices and found that the shortened weeks led to more efficient meetings, happier workers and boosted productivity by an impressive 40 per cent (Paul, 2019). While these are early findings from a workplace intervention, they match up with what we know about excessive stress. Stress reduces people's productivity rather than enhancing it, and is estimated to cost organizations billions of dollars (Bolden-Barrett, 2019).

The key principle in time management is that *there's no such thing as time management: it's all choice management*. A healthy relationship with time comes from slowing down and prioritizing. By being mindful of where you invest your attention, your energy starts to feel more in flow and less scattered. Until such time as old industrial attitudes to work adapt to the 21st century and four-day working weeks become the norm, here are a few principles that might work for you in getting more done in less time:

1 Pause

This is a counter-intuitive move if you're in the midst of chaos; the default is often to keep going when things are busy. Next time you feel caught up in busy work, take a step back and take a deep breath. You now have the opportunity to ask: *what's really needed in this moment?*

2 Batch

Switching from one task to another puts strain on your attention and energy. It's called multi-tasking, task switching or context switching – and it wastes time (Buser and Peter, 2011). That's why unsorted to-do lists are not the best tool for organization. One thing you can do is to group your tasks under different headings like health, home, relationships, creative work, admin, etc. This will allow you to focus on one area of activity and minimize the effort needed to switch from one task to another. You may also allocate your batched tasks to times of the day that work best for you; for example, creative thinking in the morning or admin on a Sunday.

3   Prioritize (have a 'not-to-do' list)

If you feel you're constantly firefighting, you're probably doing a lot of things that seem urgent but are not important or relevant (Covey, 2012). For this, I'd recommend a 'not to-do' list. Alongside batching, start moving tasks from your to-do list to your *not-to do list*. In Chapter 8 you'll get to do an energy audit to help you gain more clarity and prioritize the things that energize you and drop the things that drain you. I often recommend only focusing on one key goal at a time, giving your undivided attention to a single task.

4   Commit

Many people want to 'grow their confidence'. The trick is, however, that confidence is a *by-product of action*. Confidence is not a prerequisite for taking action. Commitment and a little courage are much more valuable than waiting for the elusive confidence to show up. If you are struggling with feelings of confidence, try focusing on committing to one small action instead – whether or not you *feel* confident. Stop overthinking – start acting.

5   Automate and delegate

Any task that is repetitive can be automated. In other words, you can put in place a system for it that doesn't require your decision-making time. This reduces your cognitive load and frees up your mind and energy to do the tasks that only you can do. Any task that could be done better or more quickly by someone else, can be delegated to them. It doesn't have to be complicated; many leaders like Steve Jobs or Barack Obama reduced cognitive load and decision-making time by minimizing wardrobe decisions and wearing a standard outfit! What can be standardized, automated or delegated in your life?

6 Focus

It's one thing to have a wealth of great ideas coming to you; it's another to sustain enough energy for its implementation over a period of time. In a VUCA world with its ever increasing distractions, practising focus will give you a real advantage (Newport, 2016). Once you have batched your tasks, resist the temptation to do too much in one go. Chunk it up. Take one small step at a time.

7 Drop it

Sometimes you'll drop the ball at work or at home. It's ok. If you don't give yourself permission for this to happen, you're going to spend more time worrying about getting things right (also known as perfectionism) and less time focused on the task in front of you (Dufu and Steinem, 2018).

If you only choose one thing, meditate

Many people feel they can't meditate. But if you can sit still and focus on a few breaths noticing your racing thoughts and heartbeat, then you have meditated. If you can't find 10 minutes a day to sit still and breathe because you're always trying to deal with a problem, then in the words of Tony Robbins, 'You don't have a *problem*. You don't have a life!' It doesn't mean that it only takes a few breaths to develop and stabilize a calm, clear, open state of mind (mindfulness). But you have a simple tool. A few minutes a day can transform your quality of life. Take a look at the evidence-based Skeptic's Guide to Meditation by Dan Harris (Harris and Happify, nd).

Meditation has been dubbed the next public health revolution (Harris, 2014). It has many benefits. Brain imaging studies have shown that it thickens the more advanced part of the brain in evolutionary terms (the neocortex) and thins out the survival focused, reactive areas (the amygdala in the midbrain). Meditation *literally* changes your brain (Ireland, 2014). People who practise mindfulness meditation for just eight weeks report improved attention, memory and general wellbeing (Frietsch, 2016).

But what is meditation exactly? Well, it's a tool to cultivate a healthy mind, one that can see clearly and doesn't get lost in psychological complexity. The fruit of meditation is mindfulness, ie a moment-to-moment awareness of what's going on inside you, and an ability to relate to it with patience, wisdom and compassion rather than from regrets over the past or anxiety about the future. It's a great tool for going through a creative cycle. By bringing awareness to your experience in the moment, you are able to see new possibilities and break free of old patterns of thought and behaviour that hold you back from fulfilling your deepest potential.

We will explore how to use this ability (mindfulness) to bring awareness to your thoughts and emotions, to transform your limiting beliefs and step into the unknown, in the next chapter. As most people find it difficult to sit and meditate, we will look at complementary alternatives to sitting on a meditation cushion: self-enquiry (questioning thoughts) and self-mastery (being with emotions) that you can practise in day-to-day life.

For now, you might want to explore the topic a bit more and do your own research. Remember that meditation doesn't have to be practised in a religious or cultural context. You can find many freely available simple practices online through universities and research institutes, like the generous selection offered free of charge by the Mindful Awareness Research Center of the University of California, Los Angeles.

MEDITATION FOR CALM AND RELAXATION

Many different types of meditation exist. For the purposes of calm and relaxation, you can start with any meditation that invites you to concentrate on one object. Usually people start with the breath. In this kind of meditation, the practice is getting you to do less (less thinking, less distraction, less reactivity) than you would normally do. Just a few moments of focus on a single object in a meditation posture will provide a sense of spaciousness and calm, which is where this type of meditation gets its name: concentration or *samatha* meditation.

However, calm and relaxation aren't the only purpose of meditation, although many people use it that way (like a stress-management technique). By paying attention to how your thoughts, feelings and sensations come and go and how they interact with each other to create states of minds (as well as identities and narratives) that shape your reality, you start to feel a sense of clarity, ease and self-trust. You start to notice the quiet gap between thoughts and make this calm, still space your new home. With practice you derive profound insights about how your mind works to create your reality (which is where this type of meditation gets its name: insight or *vipassana* meditation).

So, the ultimate purpose of meditation isn't just to relax but to cultivate a mindful quality of mind that can face anything that is real and let go of the mental fabrications that perpetuate confusion, fear and frustration. By tuning into your *inner* landscape you see the *outer* world more clearly – these are ultimately the same as far as perception is concerned. We'll come back to this in Chapter 6.

Building and maintaining healthy boundaries

If you work in a service-oriented profession like healthcare or in customer services, you're at high risk of burnout (Aronsson *et al*,

2017; Singh *et al*, 1994). The ability to see where your responsibilities end and another person's begin is tough. When you're trying to help the human being in front of you, feeling that the organization you work for might be letting them down, the boundary between their need and your resources can become blurred. This problem doesn't have an easy solution. However, what can be managed more clearly is when mission creep occurs, and you start to take on more than your fair share in your organization because you've grown a reputation for being reliable and conscientious.

In a work culture with unrealistic performance expectations, your health, relationships and, ultimately, your ability to perform can suffer. You might become increasingly short on solutions to problems you face. Most people would agree that boundaries are a good idea when there's a systematic encroachment on their time and energy, but it's harder to know what this means in practice, or to find the courage to say 'no'. Let's look at boundaries a little more closely and equip you with a few key concepts and tools.

What are boundaries?

A boundary isn't a fixed thing but a change of direction. The principle of boundaries is that *where attention goes, energy flows*. If you wake up one day to realize that your attention is being taken up in people, places and activities that aren't aligned with your values (burnout is a clue), then it's time to redirect your attention. For example, if you start to prioritize your self-care, you are naturally placing a boundary between you and other things that could drain you. You're refocusing your attention and energy. This may require that you say 'no' – or it may not. You may simply shift your commitments and schedule to align with self-care.

Conversely, breaching your own boundaries occurs when you say 'yes' to something you don't really want to do. You're effectively redirecting your attention (and energy) in a way that doesn't align with what's true for you. It may seem trivial in the moment, but the consequences on your life catch up. You can see how small decisions can have a big impact over time; for example, saying 'yes' to a small project, or one day a month sitting on a committee because it seems like a trivial commitment.

Boundaries are external and internal

Many people understand boundaries in terms of saying 'no' to demands. They also generally find it exceedingly difficult to do so. But for every demanding job, boss or partner, there's an even more demanding 'inner-boss' convincing you to say 'yes' when you want to say 'no', and making you feel guilty if you do muster a little courage to say 'no'. Boundaries have to start *inside*; for example, by giving more attention to your inner genius than to your inner boss. The inner boss is the set of fearful, highly critical thoughts that drive you hard and disconnect you from your inner genius. It also thinks it knows better than your inner genius (we'll explore this further later).

The wonderful thing about creating space to activate your higher cognitive functions, like creativity, is that you start to reconnect to your sense of what's true for you. As a result, you can make decisions that are aligned with your deeper potential (rather than being a slave to your inner boss's misguided demands). Before that happens, though, you might feel a little uncertain, so here are a couple of principles that might help.

ELIMINATE WHAT DRAINS YOU AND PRIORITIZE WHAT ENERGIZES YOU

You've probably noticed that when you're doing something because it's fun and exciting, you may feel tired, but you won't feel *drained*. You feel happy and energized. On the other hand, if you're doing something out of fear or obligation, you're much more likely to feel drained. Below are some examples of what you might say 'yes' or 'no' to.

Examples of things you might say 'no' to because they drain you:

- Projects you don't really want to do, people you don't want to see and places you don't want to go to but that you engage with out of misplaced guilt.

- Social activities that don't suit your energy level (big parties are hard on introverts, long stretches of solitude are hard on extroverts).

- Conversations based on complaints and gossip.

- Unbalanced relationships with people who expect you to do emotional labour for them (ie be a receiver for their venting or help them process their feelings without an understanding of the impact on you or of their role in creating the problem in the first place).

- Junk food (high calorie, low nutrient value).

Examples of things you might say 'yes' to because they energize you:

- Nature.
- Music.
- Exercise.
- People who honour your emotions and thought processes.
- Meditation.
- A healthy diet that nourishes you.
- Communities that support your aspirations and show you new possibilities.
- Books/writing or talks that inspire you, impart wisdom or stimulate your imagination and creative thinking.

SAY 'NO'

Saying 'no' is one of the most life-changing skills you can learn, especially if you're a people-pleaser.

When you say 'no' to something, you might feel it's final. Then a fear of missing out (FOMO) might kick in. The truth is that most decisions are reversible, so you can always have a conversation if you change your mind. It's not something to do all the time, it's just a way to take the pressure off if you're trying to navigate decisions. More often than not, when you start to say 'no' to things that drain you, you'll feel lighter.

Boundaries in a nutshell

Where attention flows energy goes.

To master the flow of your energy, master your attention (mindfulness).

Say 'yes' to things that energize you and 'no' to things that drain you.

Align your energy with your deeper potential by stilling your attention.

Resistance to slowing down

'I can't slow down – people are counting on me!'

Does this sound familiar? We touched on this earlier in the chapter, but it's a common thought process, especially for high achievers and people who derive an identity from being a rescuer. For some, it becomes a part of their identity. However, most situations are not *actually* a matter of life or death, so unless we can look at the way you set yourself up for burnout through engrained patterns of thinking and behaviour, self-care will just be a pit-stop on the way to exhaustion rather than a doorway to sustainable and fulfilling work.

Managing your inner boss: how to cope with unhelpful thought patterns

The bad boss inside your head is known by several names. Some people might call it the inner critic or gremlin. Whatever you call it, the inner boss is an interconnected set of patterns of thinking. We almost all have one. It's a composite of the ways of thinking that we have internalized during our upbringing from family, school, society, etc and that drive us to pursue goals, success and external objects in the hope that happiness will be gained. What makes it a bad boss is that it can drive us to pursue goals and 'success' even if the goals aren't actually aligned with our true values. The inner boss is fuelled by the fight-flight-freeze responses of the mammalian-reptilian brain (the more primitive part of the brain compared to the neocortex) (Longe *et al*, 2010). It's not so interested in your creative genius or your need for restoration and contemplation.

The inner boss is pretty unsophisticated. It prefers to shout, judge and make rash decisions (fast thinking) rather than consider things calmly and wisely (slow thinking). After all, its job is survival. Other features it displays:

- It likes to blow things out of proportion. It can notice a small detail like the look in someone's eyes or the tone in their voice and trigger a full-scale offensive.
- It can get into scriptwriting mode and paint you in a terrible picture in comparison to others.
- It does not enjoy the present moment for very long and even if you achieve a goal, it will create new expectations and goalposts that you need to meet.
- It favours short-term gratification over long-term contentment. It prefers the comfort zone.
- It doubts you and your capabilities.
- It uses limiting thoughts as a defence mechanism against the unknown, which it perceives as the highest threat.

So it's constantly scanning for danger and finding fault with everything! It's trying to keep you safe – but in a brutal way. It does not care very well for your deeper wellbeing or potential.

So how do you get out from under this bad boss's thumb? Decades of programmed thought patterns don't just disappear overnight. Slowing down and prioritizing self-care are just the start of a lifelong journey of growth and freedom.

The brain is a kind of energy allocation filter and will tend to favour the most energy efficient approach in order to conserve energy (Swart *et al*, 2015). Its job is to figure out where to direct your attention and energy. Under stress, the prefrontal cortex tends to shut down (eliminating higher cognitive functions) and be hijacked by the more primitive mammalian-reptilian brain. The mammalian-reptilian brain with its survival imperative defaults to fast-thinking, drawing on pre-stored patterns of response (like fight-flight-freeze) including strong emotions (like anger). Suddenly, everything can be painted as a threat and you're on tenterhooks behaving reactively and snapping at everything. Equally, your higher cognitive functions like curiosity and creative thinking tend to get switched off. They are mostly associated with the prefrontal cortex. In a moment of stress, they can be taken over by your mammalian-reptilian functions of fight-fight-freeze or reward chasing (your inner boss's agenda) in a fraction of a second.

This phenomenon has been called limbic hijack (Goleman, 1996). Your ability to reason, empathize, delay rewards and come up with wise solutions has literally been hijacked by survival instincts and strong emotions. The biggest problem is that the inner boss is so fast in how it takes over. Limbic hijack can happen in a few seconds and take several hours to abate depending on the circumstances (Goleman, 1996). Your attention isn't agile enough to detect such rapid shifts and stop them in their tracks before they cause damage, unless the quality of mindfulness or presence in the moment is developed.

This is why it's so important to slow down if you want to free yourself from the unhealthy inner boss influence. Reversing the limbic hijack and silencing the inner boss requires awareness and practice during protected time and space to start with. Eventually, you'll start to detect tiny shifts in your physiology and state of mind. You'll pick up these early signals of limbic hijack and intervene much sooner. By making time for self-care and creating quiet time you've already started creating conditions that help with this to calm your inner boss and unleash your inner genius. In the next chapter we'll explore self-enquiry and self-mastery as tools for refining your awareness of automatic patterns and letting them go.

SELF-CARE IS NOT A CRIME, IT'S A RESPONSIBILITY

When I ask any of the doctors or service-driven professionals how they feel about taking time out and taking care of themselves, they often say it feels uncomfortable. I've seen similar attitudes among professionals in other sectors including lawyers, scientists and in corporations. The common traits are being highly conscientious and wanting to help others. They are the high achievers and the rescuers who never feel they've done enough. But if we are to learn lessons from industries where staff and customers are happy and safe, then we have to embrace the need for work cultures to change. We can start by giving ourselves permission to slow down and prioritize self-care. By doing so, we activate the higher human capacities of wisdom and empathy that make life easier for ourselves and our fellow humans. We act as more responsible members of the human species!

If you've implemented some of the material in this chapter, you should start to feel more spaciousness and possibly more flow in life. Perhaps you've experienced more calm here and there and therefore better solutions. One of my clients instituted a daily walk in nature and found that her most brilliant business ideas came then. Maybe you've found that you're getting more done in less time and with less effort.

You should start seeing that the world doesn't end when you slow down or let go of a few things on your to-do list. What seem to be life and death responsibilities are almost certainly not. This is the perfect ground to go deeper into how you create your reality and break free of any limiting or distorted beliefs and identities that keep you trapped. Freedom and fulfilment are on the other side of the prison of limiting thoughts that routinely occupy far too much of our attention.

REMINDER: MAKING FRIENDS WITH TIME

1 The way we relate to time, creates or destroys time.

2 Being lost in psychological time (regrets over the past or concerns over the future) we waste real time and miss the moment.

3 There's no such thing as time management. It's choice management.

4 We all have the same 24 hours in a day. But we choose to use them differently. If your life is overwhelming or unmanageable on a chronic basis, it's time to make bold decisions and let go of a few things.

5 'Meditate an hour a day. If you don't have time, meditate two hours a day.'

6 This isn't about the amount of time you spend meditating or not. It's about the principle of slowing down when your instinct is to speed up, so creating space instead of more complexity and unmanageability in your life.

CHAPTER SIX

Unlearn your limiting beliefs

Many people are aware of the importance of lifelong learning. What most people are less aware of is the importance of *unlearning* (Bonchek, 2016; Clem and Schiller, 2016). Our thoughts shape our expectations of what's possible, how we relate to ourselves and other people and the social structures we create around us. Therefore, the assumptions we make can have a profound impact on the life we live and the world we collectively create. The good news is that you can unlearn old expectations, no matter how old you are or how far into a particular career.

Resolving the High Achiever Paradox

In Chapter 3 we looked at how high achievers might be at a disadvantage in terms of breaking out of the Success Trap. As a reminder, some of the elements of the High Achiever Paradox include:

1 The need for validation and significance while dismissing praise.
2 The need for the next challenge despite feeling tired or overwhelmed.

3 The need for more qualifications/credentials/training despite having plenty.
4 Fear of failure despite a track record of success.
5 Happiness not because of success but despite it.

If you feel stuck in your job or career (or any situation), it is likely that you are holding onto conflicting thoughts or assumptions, and that letting go of one of them is scary. For example, you might believe that you have to please everyone, while also wanting to take care of yourself. But the idea of letting people down terrifies you. Another example is that you might believe success is about having a lot of money or high status, and that money or status gives you safety. At the same time, you want more time to spend with your family or on artistic endeavours.

Now it is time to uncover some of these underlying beliefs – particularly around success, winning and goals – that are no longer useful to you. By questioning the sticky beliefs that get in the way of your flow, you can decide whether it is really true or not and consider alternative perspectives. By bringing awareness to these conflicting thoughts, beliefs or assumptions, your range of choices expands and a feeling of freedom to choose emerges – you are no longer at the behest of hidden beliefs and assumptions, you have freedom of choice. In other words, whereas before you may have blindly chased money (or any other form of success like status, fame or a particular image of a successful life), now you will be able to *choose* whether you want to do that.

Resolving the High Achiever Paradox does not mean that you have to disappoint people, let go of success or give up on money. It just means that you can have a more balanced response and make conscious choices. For example, you might take on a different job that pays less but gives you time back and exponentially increases your feelings of purpose. As a result, you create a community and your ideas spread to help others do the same. Resolving the High Achiever Paradox means that instead of winning the race and losing happiness, you will be able to tune into your natural happiness and allow things to unfold in your life from there, in a healthy and wise way.

The process may require some effort on your part to start with. Learning/unlearning requires focus and discipline to sit with your thoughts and examine them gently and honestly. In learning theory it's called 'desirable difficulty' (Druckman and Bjork, 1994). The process also brings up resistance to the uncomfortable states of mind that arise like uncertainty or facing the unknown. This is what I call 'desirable discomfort'. The effort is worthwhile because it helps you break through to a deeper understanding that ultimately serves the best of who you are.

Reality as a psychosocial construct: we mostly make it up

Society is habit. By repeating specific actions and interactions with others over time, their manner and form become a pattern and ingrained in our minds. If it results in an individual accepting rules or expectations as real, it's called habitualization (or socialization if it refers to a child learning wider social norms). This may be better illustrated in the context of relationships. Couples can get stuck in a dynamic where they repeat the same patterns because they inhabit certain roles and identities. For example, one person may be stuck in the 'damsel in distress' role and their partner in the 'rescuing knight' role. It's the same with our problematic bosses, colleagues and careers. We can get stuck in a way of being that isn't helpful.

If the result is the acceptance of an organization or institution as real, it's called institutionalization (Berger and Luckmann, 1966). For example, your organization exists in your mind as an organization and not just as a collection of people in a building because you and others (or people who came before you) agree that it is an *organization*. It's an idea that exists by ongoing consensus.

A couple of other ways sociologists have looked at this include Thomas's theorem and the concept of self-fulfilling prophesy. Thomas's theorem states that 'if humans define situations as real, they are real in their consequences'. For example, a teenager who is repeatedly given a label – like 'high achiever' – might live up to the term even though initially it was not a part of his or her temperament. With a self-fulfilling prophecy, even a false idea can become true if it is acted on. For example, you might be convinced that you won't get a job, so you don't apply or go to the interview, thereby ensuring that you don't get it (Little, 2012).

These insights from sociology don't imply that there isn't a real world out there. But they remind us to take our opinions, assumptions and culture a little more lightly than we normally would. Interestingly, a significant conceptual convergence is occurring between sociology, psychology, neuroscience, and parts of Western and Eastern philosophies. The idea that our experience, while real, is a product of our interpretation of facts rather than a fact itself is at the intersection.

Awareness: the key to freedom

Have you ever been so convinced that you were right in an argument, only to realize later that you were completely wrong? Did you admit it? If you did, then you're one of the braver humans. Most people hate being wrong and would prefer not to admit it when they are. This is how the mammalian-reptilian brain functions; it tends to reinforce its own view of life. Being right is a survival issue.

The mammalian-reptilian brain doesn't have the capacity to question what it believes. It has a databank of memories that it

UNLEARN YOUR LIMITING BELIEFS

strings together into stories and prefers to stick to them. It directs your attention towards what confirms its old stories and away from what doesn't. In psychology, it's called *attentional bias* or *confirmation bias*; your midbrain filters for information that it deems more important (*attentional bias*) and this tends to be information that confirms what you already believe (*confirmation bias*). It's what results in a self-fulfilling prophecy.

Your prefrontal cortex, on the other hand, is much more sophisticated and can question your old beliefs and assumptions by holding them lightly and mulling them over. It can examine a memory and reinterpret it. It can break down a story into its component memories, thoughts and emotions. It can also bring empathy and compassion to a painful experience and soothe you until the discomfort passes. In other words, it can expand your awareness and show you different perspectives. It can unlock different choices while calming and soothing you emotionally.

However, your mammalian-reptilian brain is older and louder than your prefrontal cortex because it houses powerful emotions and survival instincts. In a neuron-to-neuron battle, the mammalian-reptilian brain will win. It will beat the more recent functions of the prefrontal cortex and will refuse to cooperate, especially if it's agitated or excited (Goleman, 1996). This is the limbic hijack we mentioned in the last chapter; it clouds your ability to see other perspectives and possibilities. It tends to focus your awareness on one small thing and cut you off from the bigger picture.

It's difficult to describe awareness. It's easier to explain it in terms of the things that you're *aware of*. For example, self-awareness is the localized sense of 'you' experiencing thoughts and emotions. On the other hand, awareness in the broadest sense is centreless. You could call this centreless awareness consciousness.

So for practical purposes, we'll talk about *self*-awareness: the awareness of a 'you' experiencing thoughts and emotions moment to moment. With enough practice you can separate between the sense of a 'you' experiencing passing thoughts and emotions, and just the experience of passing thoughts and emotions itself (with no sense of a 'you' involved), which feels lighter and freer.

Your ability to notice your thoughts and emotions without taking them too seriously or being too critical is a super-power. It's also known as the quality of mind called *mindfulness*. With this kind of self-awareness, you can observe the mammalian-reptilian brain's constant interpretation of your current experience in the light of past experience. You also start to notice that you can redirect your attention from one thought or memory to another. Your self-awareness enables you to respond from a fresh perspective rather than an old one. With practice this starts to deactivate neural pathways (habits of thoughts and behaviour) that no longer serve and lay down new ones. This flexibility of attention and habit modification is the key to change.

Levels of self-awareness

Let's map out the different levels of awareness so you can have idea of where you are and work from there:

1 **Low/no self-awareness**: you are trapped in old patterns of thoughts/reactive emotions and can feel stuck in an identity like the imposter or rescuer. You can't see that the thoughts and emotions are just passing, and you tend to get lost in them.
2 **Intermediate self-awareness**: you're able to notice patterns of thought/reactive emotions but can't quite stop them.
3 **High self-awareness**: you notice old patterns/reactive emotions as they start to arise. You can stop them in their tracks before the thoughts proliferate into stories and identities or the emotions get too intense. You can act more spontaneously based on your wisdom in the moment. Your critical inner boss is quiet. You experience a sense of freedom and flow in life including through its ups and downs.

Expanding self-awareness

The transformational property of self-awareness comes from its ability to evolve old beliefs, assumptions, identities and narratives so you can break out of ones that no longer serve you. Changing your relationship to your thoughts (by bringing awareness to them and not taking them too seriously as absolutes) gives you the ability to change the thoughts themselves. This has a dramatic impact on the way you see the world, the way you feel and the actions you take subsequently.

Expanding your self-awareness simply means that you *notice what is going on better*. The faster you notice your reactions and emotions and the more granular your awareness of what's going on inside you, the less likely you are to be blinded by a biased, filtered view of the situation; you can become trapped in an emotional reaction and cause damage to a situation, relationship or your health.

This works even for notoriously addictive behaviours. One study showed that expanding awareness around smoking habits (the thoughts, feelings and behaviours that make up the habit) using basic mindfulness (self-awareness) doubled the likelihood of quitting smoking (Brewer *et al*, 2011). Being mindful or self-aware made the study participants very aware of the chain reaction of events that leads them to lighting a cigarette.

It starts with a small stressful trigger leading to the craving for a cigarette. Bringing awareness to the smoking habit also revealed to them the unpleasant aspects of smoking and amplified the sense that they were injecting harmful chemicals into their bodies, an aspect that had gone under their attentional radar until then because they weren't paying attention to it, ie being mindful. Through self-awareness they were able to rebalance the *pros* and *cons* of smoking and this appeared to deactivate the craving for a cigarette.

By analogy, through self-awareness we can become cognizant of how patterns of thinking and behaving trap us in the perceived rewards of a particular job or career while ignoring the cost to our health, relationships and opportunities to fulfil our deeper potential.

The High Achiever Paradox Transformation (HAPI) process

Self-awareness can be accessed at any time and any place, and applied to your thoughts, your emotions or both through the combination of two self-awareness tools:

1 **Self-enquiry**: bringing awareness to your limiting thoughts and questioning their validity. This helps you transform beliefs, narratives and identities that trap you. They become ideas rather than facts. It keeps your inner genius free to show you new ideas and possibilities to respond to any situation.
2 **Self-mastery**: bringing awareness to your emotions and sensations (the energy in your body). Some call it self-regulation. This helps you tolerate or even embrace intense emotions like anger or grief while shortening their duration and minimizing their negative impact on yourself and others.

SELF-AWARENESS MODEL

You may have worked out that we've explored a simple model of human consciousness. See Figure 6.1 for an illustration. For an in-depth exploration of the latest science and philosophy of consciousness, including their relationship to mindfulness practices as well as the practical implications for human happiness, I highly recommend philosopher and neuroscientist Sam Harris's book *Waking Up: A guide to spirituality without religion* (Harris, 2014).

FIGURE 6.1 Self-awareness model

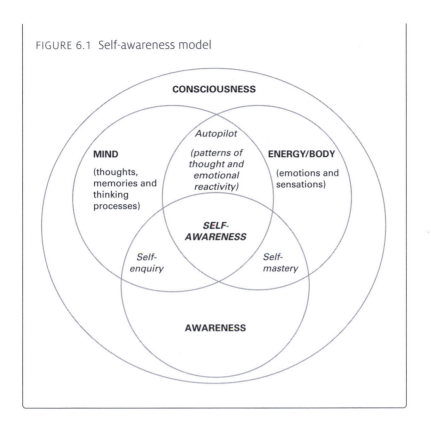

Self-enquiry: working with thoughts, narratives and identities that trap (reflect)

Learning theory tells us that in order to learn something new, you have to let go of – or at the very least question – some of the old facts and perspectives you hold. You need to unlearn, in order to learn (Newstrom, 1983). Self-enquiry is a process whereby you're noticing the thoughts that occupy your mind and rather than taking them for granted, you draw out the underlying assumptions. You acknowledge your perspective and then you check its validity by going a level deeper and identifying the hidden assumptions of your perspective.

An important aspect is that you also reveal where the contradictions between different thoughts might be, so you can resolve any inner conflict you're experiencing over whether to leave a job or take on a project, for example. By digging into this you're able to let go of fixed assumptions about unhelpful identities until you experience yourself as a coherent whole.

Restructuring your thinking is a process of patiently exploring, pruning, linking and transforming assumptions (rather than simply adding new facts). It does not have to be hard or argumentative and is much easier if you turn your need for answers into curiosity. With practice, the joy of discovery helps the process unfold effortlessly.

BEGINNER'S MIND: OPENNESS AND CURIOSITY AS ANTIDOTES TO HARMFUL THOUGHTS, IDENTITIES AND NARRATIVES

To unlearn old beliefs and break out of your limitations, you must be prepared to let go of what you think you already know and be curious and open-minded. Curiosity has been shown to be critical, not only in classroom learning but also for adult learning and optimal performance in the work place (Reio and Wiswell, 2000). The concept of having a beginner's mind goes a little further still. It is a Zen concept, describing a freedom from any preconception – your mind is free of past concepts that label and box things, and is open to exploring things afresh. Unlike curiosity, there is no active desire to learn. It's more of an openness to what is and has been described as an absence of any motive or prior agenda: a willingness to entertain all possibilities without any preference. This quality of openness in meeting with the world is discussed in the book *Zen Mind, Beginner's Mind* and is at the heart of mindfulness (Suzuki *et al*, 1970). In Western thought, this attitude is captured in the Socratic Paradox: 'I know that I know nothing'.

Another way to put it is: stay curious and never take anything for granted. A beginner's mind will keep you connected to creative ideation and help you come up with innovative solutions. It will also help you with self-enquiry. It doesn't mean that you have to give everything prolonged attention. Your openness to experience can be balanced with a willingness to discard unhelpful ideas, thoughts and assumptions rapidly.

SELF-ENQUIRY WITH FIVE QUESTIONS

Self-enquiry helps you break through deeply ingrained, unhelpful narratives about who you are, what's possible and the meaning of success. By asking a few simple questions, you can bring to light any limiting belief and break it down so that it doesn't hold you back from fulfilling your potential. One of the most easily accessible versions of this self-directed process of self-enquiry is the work of Byron Katie which, while commercially available, seems to have some evidence to back it up (Smernoff *et al*, 2015). Below is a version I have developed and used for myself and with my own clients with significant psychological shifts occurring and positive feedback. The best thing is to test it yourself and see if it helps.

You can do this alone, or with a partner who reads the questions out to you. It's very important that you do this slowly and allow the answers to arise in their own time. It's easy to try to rush in to give what may seem to be the right answer. If you answer too quickly, it's probably your inner boss trying to push you to get things done too quickly. Give yourself time to connect with your deeper thoughts and emotions.

Start simply. Bring to mind a situation you want to change at work or in your life. Take yourself back to that situation through your imagination and answer the questions:

Question 1: What thoughts and feelings are you experiencing?
   a What are your fears, frustrations and emotions about the situation? *(I'm angry at John because he didn't acknowledge my work)*
   b What are your desires and needs so that you can be happy with the situation? *(I want John to acknowledge my work)*
   c What are your expectations in this situation? *(John should acknowledge my work)*
   d What judgements are you holding? *(John is so self-centred and selfish!)*
   e What's your worst-case scenario? *(John fails to ever notice how much work I do and doesn't appreciate my value)*

Question 2: How does this thought not serve you?
- Pick one simple statement from your answers to Question 1. You can work with all of them, but do it one at a time.

Question 3: Do you choose to believe this thought? (yes/no – either is fine)
- Notice what happens whether you choose *yes* or *no* (the thoughts and feelings that arise, the actions you want to take or not take, any sense of peace or lightness).

Question 4: What's the alternative thought (that's as true or truer than the statement you're working with)?
- Reframe: Take a statement from your answers to Question 1 and reframe it until you experience clarity. For example, say the opposite: *John should not acknowledge my work*; or *I should acknowledge my work*.
- Evidence: Why could this reframe be true? Think like a scientist investigating a hypothesis – it may or may not be true, eg *I've acknowledged my own work before and it helped. By acknowledging my work, others also noticed what I had contributed and acknowledged it, too.*

Question 5: What do you resolve in this moment?
- Stay connected to a sense of openness, and welcome everything including your worst-case scenario, eg *I am willing for John not to acknowledge my work again.* Notice any shifts in your state. This is an invitation to fearlessness by preparing for inevitable setbacks as we work through a limiting belief. The Roman Stoics called it *premeditatio malorum* (Irvine, 2009).

START A JOURNAL

If you don't already have one, it's a good time to start a journal to capture the thoughts that you might like to work with. By putting your thoughts on paper first thing in the morning, or when your mind is starting to race when you're feeling upset, you'll have

---

plenty of material to work with. Capturing thoughts on paper has been shown to facilitate psychological wellbeing, creative expression (Martin-Cuellar, 2018) as well as athletic performance (Noetel *et al*, 2019), and in terms of self-enquiry, writing down stressful thoughts will help you clear your mind and see in more detail where you might be sabotaging yourself or feeling blocked.

CASE STUDY   The busy consultant who said 'no'

Freya is an extremely knowledgeable and passionate academic, public speaker and educator. Frustrated with the slow pace of change, she decided to create her own consultancy. As her work grew, the level of feeling overwhelmed became unmanageable. She had recently delivered a big project for a company and was now looking forward to focusing on her bigger mission. But they wanted her to do more and implement a strategic plan. She didn't know how to refuse.

Belief: I can't say 'no'

Here's an example of a conversation I'd have with clients addressing this kind of belief.

Question 1: What thoughts and feelings are you experiencing?
- I'm afraid that I'm going to let people down and ruin my professional relationships if I say 'no' to this project. As I step into more consulting work, I'd like to maintain good relationships.
- Saying 'no' is risky. I can't say 'no'.

Question 2: How does the thought 'I can't say "no"' not serve you?
- Believing 'I can't say "no"' doesn't serve me because: 1) it keeps me stuck in projects I don't like; 2) it makes me anxious because I'm not true to myself; 3) it stops me from suggesting alternatives that might work for others as well as me.

Question 3: Do you choose to believe it? (yes/no – either is fine)
- No. I can see that the belief is blocking me for the wrong reasons!

Question 4: What's an alternative thought and how might it be true?
- The opposite statement is, *I can say 'no!'*

- Evidence that I can say 'no' includes: 1) I've done it before; 2) people often don't mind when I've turned something down; 3) if I don't say 'no' to this I'll be even more overwhelmed and have no time for my business and family.

Question 5: What do you resolve in this moment?

- I'm willing to say 'no'. I'm open to being revisited by the limiting thought 'I can't say "no"' because that's my cue to pause and question the thought.

Freya gave herself permission to turn down the project. Emboldened by this experience of successfully saying 'no', she made a proposal to her employer to cut back her work to three days a week and it was accepted. This gave her the time to pick up new consulting projects that were much more aligned with her values, speak at international conferences and get back to writing her book. Ultimately, she found that in the space she'd created by saying 'no' things fell into place more easily and she was recruited to a great role in an educational institution that played to her talents and strengths.

CASE STUDY The doctor who let go of the need to have all the answers

Belief: I need to have the answer now

Tara, a highly specialized doctor in one of the country's top hospitals, was unsure whether to leave her job or not. She'd trained long and hard, and worked in one of the most competitive specialties, caring for children requiring complex medical and surgical treatment. She had exceeded all family expectations of success, breaking through barriers of what was expected of a woman in her culture of origin. She'd married a very supportive partner and had a child. But she was stressed by the pressures of the job and felt that she didn't receive the respect or support that she needed to perform well. The idea of leaving to try something new was tempting but also horrifying to her as she loved the specialty and had trained so hard for it.

Through transformational enquiry she uncovered a limiting thought that was causing her stress at work and at home:

Question 1: What thoughts and feelings are you experiencing?

- I'm believing that I need to know the answer now.

Question 2: How is the thought *'I need to know the answer now'* not serving you?

- It feels stressful and makes me feel inadequate because I can't know all the answers all the time.
- It cuts me off from my creative ideas and ability to find better solutions to problems.
- It perpetuates an unhealthy culture where doctors pretend to know the answers, which can harm patients.

Question 3: Do you choose to believe that thought?

- No. But I can feel that I'm really attached to this belief. I really think that I must have the answer immediately under pressure and in emergency situations. At the same time, I can see that it's not realistic and that it's not helpful to patients if I'm so focused on my own stress when I'm trying to help patients.

Question 4: What's an alternative thought and why might it be true?

- I suppose I don't have to know the answer all the time.
- Why? I remember a stressful situation where I took a step back and gave myself time to figure things out. Eventually, I had an intuition about a patient's diagnosis. I didn't mention it, but I can see that next time it would be useful to take this approach. On another occasion, I decided to let go of the need to make a perfect presentation of a clinical case. I was going to stay late and not see my child that evening but decided to go home. The meeting went fine, and it turned out that the level of detail I originally thought I needed to go into wasn't that useful for the patient's care!
- Another alternative thought is: *They need to know the answer now*. Why might this be true? It's true that colleagues or bosses may put pressure on me to give them an answer. That's because they're putting pressure on themselves or someone else to have the answer. But if it's not available immediately, that's not something I (or they) can do much about in that moment. By taking a step back and asking whether this information is absolutely necessary, everyone gets to feel a bit calmer and think more clearly and effectively about a plan.

Question 5: What do you resolve in this moment?

I'm willing not to know the answers all the time. Next time I start thinking, 'I need to know the answer now', I'll know it's a signal to take a step back from the stress and frenzy around me and think clearly.

By going through this self-enquiry, Tara was also able to see that her career decision was not an emergency. She found it freeing to know that she didn't need to have the answer to her career move immediately and could give herself time and space to figure it out. She could start to see that not knowing the answers didn't make her a fraud, imposter or failure, it just made her human.

Self-mastery: working with emotions (release)

Working with limiting beliefs can be emotional. There's much more than an intellectual conversation going on. After all, we're talking about rewiring your brain. Asking the five questions in the self-enquiry above can look easy on the surface, but it can be emotionally challenging when done correctly and with focused, calm attention. The answers to the self-enquiry process may unfold over days, weeks or months, if it's a very old belief you picked up as a child, or if it's deeply ingrained in the culture. You may need to take a break from the process and come back to it. Bringing awareness to the emotions and tension that come up during self-enquiry is the other wing of the HAPI process.

A universal and yet often overlooked fact is that all emotions pass. It doesn't feel like it when you're in the thick of it. But their life-cycle can be lengthened or shortened through self-awareness – this is self-mastery. It can be impossible to stay angry or upset for very long as you allow each emotion to go through its natural cycle without getting lost in it by proliferating narratives around it. As a general principle, imagine what it would be like if you could cut down the length of time you feel angry, frustrated or lonely in life? How would your quality of life improve? What would you do with the extra time and energy? Imagine the positive impact on your relationships and the possibilities that would become available to you in work and life. The benefit to your happiness is hard to overestimate.

So, if you feel tense or anxious during self-enquiry, that's often a good sign – you're hitting on something important. As you unlearn old ways of thinking about the world, part of you (your inner boss) will resist the change and you might feel sad about it for a while. But with patience and acceptance, this emotional cycle of change can occur naturally and last no less and no more than it needs to (Moran and Lennington, 2013).

Let's say you decide to go for your dream to create your own business. You might start off hopeful and optimistic (uninformed optimism), then start to realize what's involved and how long it will take to get going (informed pessimism), then you hit the 'messy middle' (perhaps you've already quit your job and can't go back but the business isn't quite working yet and you have no idea what else you could do). Here most people give up or get stuck in a loop. The risk of limbic hijack and giving into survival fears is high. But if you handle the messy middle well, for example with gentle self-enquiry to release any limiting thoughts, you eventually get through to the other side as you start to see your business working or a new role appears that works much better for you, like Freya in the example above (this is completion of the cycle). This emotional cycle of change model has parallels with the stages of learning model (Flower, 1999) and the transformational learning model (Boyd and Myers, 1988).

THE 'MESSY MIDDLE'

You may recognize the uncomfortable phase of change (its uncertainty and confusion) under different names. Vulnerability researcher and leadership trainer Brené Brown calls it 'the dense fog of uncertainty'. You may have heard it called by different names:

- the unknown unknown;
- the space between stories;

- the valley of despair;
- the dark night of the soul;
- the bardo;
- the dark cave of change;
- the liminal space;
- the shadowland.

This is where you're most susceptible to limbic hijack, and where your self-awareness is really going to help you navigate the situation and not give up. It will help you see that you've gone from an open-minded (beginner's mind) mode to a narrow-minded one. You may also notice that the thoughts in your mind are multiplying and rather critical: 'this won't work', 'you don't know what you're doing', 'you're an idiot', etc. These are all beliefs you can put through the five questions of self-enquiry.

RELEASING INTENSE EMOTIONS: BREATHE AND SOOTHE

If you're going through a tough time, self-soothing is a key skill. Rather than toughing it out by pushing yourself harder or criticizing yourself, you take an attitude of *attending and befriending* the contents of your mind at any one moment, bringing a soothing quality to how you deal with things.

Self-soothing can be counter-intuitive for high achievers, who are often highly self-critical. However, new interventions emerge as the evidence grows. For example, Compassion-Focused Therapy is a clinical intervention with soothing as a key component and developed specifically for people who are exceedingly self-critical. A review of its benefits are promising (Leaviss and Uttley, 2015). We also know that the oxytocin released with self-soothing and self-compassion promotes feelings of trust, safety and generosity (Uvnäs-Moberg *et al*, 2014).

The importance of compassion alongside clarity of mind in personal transformation has been known for millennia. In certain forms of Buddhism, for example, loving-kindness meditation and compassion meditation are important practices. In a short space of time, loving-kindness meditation promotes positive emotion, feelings of belonging and social connection while curbing negative thoughts and feelings (Hofmann *et al*, 2011). Here are a few techniques to help you move through the intense emotions of transformation. They will counter the activation of the limbic hijack and neutralize the fight-flight-freeze response.

1 Breathe deeply and mindfully

Take time to focus only on your breath and count to 10 if you can. Rest your attention on a part of your body that feels the movement of the breath and notice the rhythm.

2 Soothing self-talk and visualization

Gently repeat a simple phrase like, 'I'm ok'. If you can do this, visualize different people involved in a challenging situation and allow them to be OK too. It doesn't matter what role they play in the situation or how they're upsetting you. You can alternate between: 'I'm ok' and 'they're ok'. If this works for you, you might like to try the loving-kindness meditation. You can find free versions online from universities or research institutes.

3 Spend time in nature

Spending time in nature reconnects you to your senses and slows down your mind. It can give you an experience of beauty and connection as well as a sense of vastness and acceptance that allows you to release emotions through tears or letting out a scream, for example. A review of the effects of walking in forests showed that it reduced anxiety and depression as well as improving heart and lung health (Oh *et al*, 2017).

4 Self-acknowledgement and gratitude

This is a powerful exercise. You're essentially giving yourself a compliment by recognizing the good things you're doing.

You can use a simple phrase like: *I acknowledge myself for my courage*. It's similar to a gratitude exercise but it's easier. Practising gratitude is known to have many benefits for wellbeing and relationships, but gratitude can be hard to access when you're going through a really hard time (Bono *et al*, 2012). Other forms of this include affirmations like: 'I am brave and wise' as well as positive self-talk in the third person that encourages and advises like: 'you've done this before, you can do it again' (Kross *et al*, 2014).

5 Stretching and exercise

Bringing awareness to the basic sensations and areas of tension in your body can help to move the sensations around and dissipate the tension. Yoga is an excellent practice, but there are many other forms of mindful physical activity like qigong or taichi. Physical activity also releases endorphins that help you feel good.

6 Meditation for insight and clarity

Mindfulness is defined as the ability to pay attention, on purpose, to the present moment without judgement. The result is that your self-awareness becomes increasingly refined. You can notice smaller and smaller elements of your experience as specific sensations and minor shifts in mood. The advantage is that you can free yourself from an automatic thought pattern, identity or emotion much more quickly – before you say or do something you may regret.

Seven shifts you'll experience with the HAPI process

The reason the self-enquiry captured in the five questions seems to work is because it loosens the hold that an old identity has on you – you unlearn your old self. It doesn't necessarily replace your identity with a new one, it simply allows you to see the multiple identities you can inhabit and be aware of a wider range of possibilities and choices in life.

Here are seven key things you may notice as you stay in this enquiry process. You will find it easier to:

1 respond to any problem or situation safely with authenticity and integrity;
2 challenge the limiting identity and beliefs triggered by the situation;
3 discover and understand a key decision (a belief that was chosen) sometime in the past as a result of a similar situation;
4 notice the identity/belief's negative consequences and ramifications over time;
5 notice the possibilities of loosening the identity/belief and new opportunities as a result;
6 release emotions and cycle through the experience of change as well as gather the freed up energy and use it to act differently;
7 take more spontaneous and creative action and let go of attachment to the outcome.

As you practise, refinements can be made to how you enquire into your limiting beliefs and the level of compassion you bring to them expanded. You may also notice some deeper principles of psychological transformation emerge including:

- Thoughts aren't fixed.
- Emotions always pass.
- A better thought creates a better emotion.
- If you're going to tell a story make it a good one.
- If you're going to wear an identity, remember to take it off.
- You're more than your thoughts, emotions, narratives and identities.
- Self-awareness is your home.
- Awareness is freedom.

When we have self-awareness, we have a new psychological home free of identities, narratives and beliefs. We can access it anytime and feel calm and happy regardless of what's going on outside us.

We can dip in and out of identities as needed. From here it's easier to redefine who we are and make better choices. It's also easier to take risks because no matter the outcome you know you're fine. You can just come back to your self-awareness home.

Now we've gone into the deep work, you will have new insights to play with and perhaps have a few ideas or a vision to guide your next steps. In the next chapter we'll look at some additional, practical tools to complement the core process.

PART THREE

Thriving outside the trap

CHAPTER SEVEN

Practical freedom

Tools to reconnect, respond and receive

In the last section of the book, you slowed down, created space and explored how to break free of limiting beliefs and narratives using the HAPI process. You'll have considered the thoughts and emotions that drive your behaviours. You may have begun to resolve your version of the High Achiever Paradox, by unlearning old beliefs that don't serve you anymore, so you can break free of any version of success that isn't authentically yours.

This may have led you to new insights and inspiration about what you might want to do next.

This chapter will take you through the second part of the Creative Cycle. You get to draw on the insights you've gained by reconnecting to the things you really care about (Reconnect); taking skilful action and influencing outcomes without manipulation or pressure (Respond); and being patient with factors outside your control while celebrating and acknowledging the small victories (Receive).

AFFIRMATIONS AND POSITIVE THINKING

Do you use affirmations or positive thinking? If you have, you may have felt an increase in your confidence and self-esteem. It may have helped you to improve your health, lose weight or get a promotion. But how long did the good feeling last? How often did the affirmations lead to action and how long did any change last?

When people engage in positive thinking – like visualizing their dream future – on its own, the evidence shows that they are less likely to take action or overcome obstacles (Oettingen, 2014; Vohs *et al*, 2017) than those who use a deeper process like self-enquiry and self-mastery. Recent psychological research suggests that obstacle elimination (seeing and addressing the perceived obstacles to success) is more energizing and effective than motivating yourself to achieve goals through positive thinking (Oettingen and Reininger, 2016; Cross and Sheffield, 2019; Chowdhury, 2020). For people to really engage with the possibilities in their lives and take action, they need to face reality head on and engage with the perceived obstacles. So, while it's a good thing to have a destination in mind, knowing what's in the way is as important – if not more so. Therefore, you can always start with your limiting thoughts.

Reconnect: mission, purpose and values

Mission and purpose

Having a mission statement is ubiquitous in organizations these days (Morphew and Hartley, 2006). In modern, secular societies, the imperative to have a mission or purpose (and clear goals) has spilled over to individuals. You may have felt that you need to have one yourself.

The concepts of mission and purpose are linked, and the words are used interchangeably here. To keep it simple, it's the thing you believe you were meant to do, or the reason you get up in the morning. It's easy to get caught up in trying to find a big mission or purpose, but let's look at the assumptions behind this first.

CASE STUDY   The lawyer who let go of the need to have a purpose

Belief: I need to know my purpose

A lawyer felt frustrated that she couldn't figure out her purpose, and felt she was wasting time in her career and life.

Question 1: What thoughts and feelings are you experiencing?

- I should know my purpose.

Question 2: How does this thought not serve you?

- It makes me feel inadequate and lacking.
- It puts a break on my motivation and I procrastinate.
- It creates a new problem for me to worry about.

Question 3: Do you choose to believe it? (yes/no – either is fine)

- No, I choose not to believe that anymore.
- How does that feel? I feel lighter. I see that there are things I want to do that I can start immediately without knowing my purpose. Perhaps that is my purpose, to do the next thing that feels right without thinking about it too much.

Question 4: What's the alternative thought (that's as true or truer than the statement you're working with)?

- I don't need to know my purpose.
- Why might this be true? When I was younger, I didn't think about my purpose and I still did things that I enjoyed and that felt meaningful. When I don't worry about knowing my purpose and trust myself, I seem to just get on with what I want to do. It's easier to spot new opportunities and take them up.

Question 5: What do you resolve in this moment?

• I don't need to know my purpose right now. I'm open to being where I am and to new experiences. I'm also open to getting obsessed with finding my purpose again because that's my cue to slow down and question my thoughts in that moment.

Questioning limiting assumptions and beliefs doesn't just facilitate action, it enables us to reveal what it is that we really care about and want to devote our energy to. If you're stuck trying to find your purpose and procrastinating on taking a leap or making a decision, question the assumptions you're making – do you really need to know your purpose before taking a step?

Values

Values are helpful if you know what they mean. They help you prioritize and feel integrity when you live by them. Perhaps you've been taken through training exercises or handed a list of values to choose from and identify your top ones. But like mission statements and purpose, they've been subjected to the goal-oriented tyranny of having to find them. Organizations will name their values as: people, service, innovation, etc as part of a corporate exercise, but they may ring hollow when they're just handed down to you. Similarly, on an individual level, without really understanding what values are or giving yourself enough time to uncover them, they can just be a stick to beat yourself with.

Values are simply what you truly care about or the things that have *positive emotional valence* for you. It's helpful to know what you care about, because then you can be in alignment and feel a sense of fulfilment as you focus on things that energize you. There's overlap between values, needs and desires; some of what you care about is a result of your past conditioning and upbringing. So to identify your deepest values, a process of self-enquiry is the way forward. It requires patience and deep listening. If you treat finding values as another goal, you're at risk of confirmation bias: you might choose values that keep you comfortable and reflect external expectations. It doesn't have to be a difficult intellectual exercise. Your values (like purpose and mission) can effortlessly reveal themselves as a by-product of the inner clarity that emerges once you've challenged your limiting beliefs and narratives.

Ultimately, we share universal values like happiness. But we may also have individual preferences. One person may have an emphasis on freedom while for another it's on belonging. Values may also change over time and that's ok. Give yourself permission to be completely authentic. Giving yourself permission to value what you value is liberating.

Tools to reconnect

Here are some tools you could use to reconnect with your purpose, mission and values. If an answer comes up that's unexpected or uncomfortable, just write it down. You can always put it through self-enquiry to see what's going on underneath. Seeing the articulation of your purpose as a creative process, rather than a goal-oriented one, will likely give you much better results and help you learn much more about yourself.

EPITAPH

The harder you try to come up with a mission or purpose, the less likely you are to come upon it. Try using your imagination instead. Think of your purpose as an epitaph in the present tense and ask *what would I like to be remembered for?* For example, 'I want to be remembered for writing music that delights the heart and inspires people to be their best selves'. It doesn't have to be grandiose. It can be as simple as, 'I want to be remembered for raising a loving family'.

IKIGAI

Ikigai is a Japanese concept meaning 'reason for being' (García, 2017). It equates your purpose with the sweet spot at the intersection of four factors:

1 what you love doing;
2 what you're good at (preferably your zone of genius);
3 what the world needs;
4 what people will pay for.

Working in your zone of genius is more likely to create fulfilment and flow – see Gay Hendricks' 2009 book *The Big Leap*. According to him, most people build successful careers in their zone of excellence (learned skills), but this can ultimately lead to dissatisfaction. The zone of genius uses their innate gifts. The zone of genius allows for consistent inspiration, coming up with work that is unique, and excelling far and beyond what anyone else is doing (Wiest, 2018).

Going through the *Ikigai* exercise is likely to bring up a range of limiting beliefs and narratives that you have the tools to address from Chapter 6. If you're thinking that you don't have a zone of genius, I would certainly invite you to question that thought!

CONNECTING TO A SENSE OF PURPOSE

To avoid getting caught up in the chase for Purpose with a capital P, you can focus on purpose with a small p – fulfilling your purpose one moment at a time. What is true for you in this moment? What would you happily do in this moment? That's your purpose for now.

For your big purpose, engage with your creativity. Go and sit in nature with a journal. Allow yourself to daydream or get lost in your surroundings. Note any memories of what you loved doing as a child or at a younger age. Hold space for these memories and any ideas that come out of that space. Write about them, explore

---

them further, share them with others who support you. This is a gentle process that's more like gardening than mathematical modelling. Give time for the seeds to sprout and nurture them away from harsh criticism or premature expectations. If a thought comes that feels stressful or limiting, apply the HAPI process.

Purpose: pitfalls and litmus test

PITFALLS WITH PURPOSE

These are when you expect too much of your purpose, too quickly (watch out for your inner boss); or when you are coming from a place of despair or neediness; or when you are making it about saving others or saving the world (watch out for the rescuer).

LITMUS TEST

Speaking your purpose feels enlivening and heart opening. But it may also evoke fear. It should feel a little bit exciting and a little bit scary but that you're willing to face the challenges. Test it by saying it out loud. See how it lands with people who support you and what they reflect back.

Respond: taking responsibility for your time, energy, communication and influence

Being free to choose what to do with your career can be daunting to start with. The fear that holds high achievers back the most is probably *fear of failure*. Here are a few other common fears, particularly if you decide to take on more leadership or work independently:

- I'm afraid of not knowing what to do.
- I'm afraid of not having any structure.

- I'm afraid of being lonely.
- I'm afraid of not making enough money.

Addressing these universal limiting thoughts and narratives will help you find your own unique solutions. The next case study gives an example of what happened when Antiope, a busy GP, was finding it challenging to allocate time and energy to her self-care and passion projects. She was in firefighting mode with no end in sight.

CASE STUDY The GP who didn't want to let people down

Question 1: What thoughts and feelings are you experiencing?

- I really feel that I mustn't let people down.

Question 2: How does the thought 'I mustn't let people down' not serve you?

- It puts me under pressure to keep everyone happy.
- It stops me from focusing on what I need to stay calm and happy myself.
- It cuts me off from my bigger purpose.
- I let people down anyway because I'm not truly available if I'm always busy.

Question 3: Do you choose to believe it? (yes/no – either is fine)

- No, I choose not to believe it (although I notice that it's hard to let it go completely).
- How does it feel? I'm mostly relieved.

Question 4: What's the alternative thought (that's as true or truer than the statement you're working with)?

- Alternative 1: People mustn't let me down.
- Why might that be true? I deserve support as much as anyone else. It feels freeing. If I do it all and burnout, it doesn't work.

- Alternative 2: I must let people down! I've been trying hard for so long, it's time for a break! It's unrealistic to think I can please everyone, so it's inevitable that I have to let some people down. They may not even be that disappointed. It's just in my head.

Question 5: What do you resolve in this moment?

- I'm open to feeling that I let people down because I need to adjust my expectations of myself until I find a better balance. I'm willing to feel the pressure of 'I mustn't let people down' again, because that's my cue to question my thinking in that moment.

Tools to respond: time and energy

If you're able to uncover the limiting thoughts and narratives that lead you to misallocate your time, you'll notice that you've freed up more time. You're less caught up in anxiety about the past or future. Here are a few practical tools to stay aware of how you're allocating your time and energy and align the allocation with your values.

YOUR PERSONAL ENERGY AUDIT

Your time and energy are finite. In a culture where being overwhelmed and busy-ness are the norm, most people struggle with their energy levels. The impact of cultural and individual level assumptions like 'keeping busy is good' and the role of the inner boss (or inner critic) have been discussed in the previous chapters. As a general rule, misalignment between your values and actions is draining.

Your personal energy audit is a tool to help you differentiate what energizes you from what drains you and do more of what energizes you and less of what drains you to restore and maintain your energy balance. I learned this from my coach (Litvin, nd). Buildings undergo energy audits to ensure they're maintained properly and prevent energy leaks, and so can we.

Draw a line down a piece of paper and label one column: *What drains me* and the other *What energizes me*. Think of the past week or month. List the people, places and habits that you engaged with in the appropriate column. Keep going until you feel you've captured as much as you can. Now look at the column of things that drain you: what can you do less of or let go of entirely? Conversely, looking at the column of things that energize you: what can you do more of? If you find that it's hard to let go of what drains you, a limiting belief may be operating that you can explore.

YOUR IDEAL AVERAGE DAY

If you know what energizes you and what drains you, your day can be planned accordingly. The ideal average day can be used to imagine what kind of career or job would work for you best. It's also helpful if you're unsure about your purpose or big mission. If you struggle with the question 'where do you see yourself in five years?', the ideal average day may work better for you.

Here are a few questions you can start with when designing your ideal average day:

- What kind of activities, people and places do you want in your diary?
- What kind of activities, people and places do you NOT want in your diary?
- What are the best times for you for creative thinking, planning or meetings?
- How do you feel at the end of the day?
- Who do you review and celebrate your day with?

You may also want to borrow from highly creative entrepreneurs who differentiate between 'manager days' where many tasks are scheduled including meetings, versus 'maker days' where long stretches of quiet time are scheduled to facilitate creative thinking (Graham, 2009).

YOUR APPOINTMENT WITH YOURSELF: PERSONALIZED REGULAR REVIEWS

If you work in an organization, you may be familiar with annual reviews that most people dread or feel indifferent to. You can take charge of your own review. Use it to your advantage for self-accountability. You can also use it to celebrate your commitment, courage and results.

Google's Director of Executive Coaching and Leadership provides a framework that spans a daily minute to a decadal review (Peterson, 2010).

Here are some of the questions that you can play with as you design your own system:

- What did I create today?
- Did I complete what I intended?
- If not, what held me back? What limiting narrative came into play? How did I make excuses (look into these to avoid repeating the pattern)?
- Is this task/idea still important to me?
- Without the narrative holding me back, what becomes possible?
- What would I need to say 'no' to in order to say 'yes' to what's true for me?
- What would I need to say 'yes' to in order to say 'no' to what holds me back?
- How and when will I take action?
- Am I coming from a place of openness/service or fear/neediness?
- Where did I act from autopilot rather than self-awareness?
- What am I grateful for?

You may find this kind of scrutiny uncomfortable at first and that's ok. You can use just one question: *What have I created recently?* The idea is to design your own accountability system.

Tools to respond: communication and influence

Never underestimate your influence. Your body language says more as you walk into a room than your words, and your words often carry the energy of your body language. Being aware of your state of mind and what story you may be telling yourself will give you more of a grasp of how people are responding to you. (Intentional) influence is a key leadership skill in the VUCA world where no one has all the answers or all the power (Barton *et al*, 2012). But you don't need an executive title to influence in your organization.

Influence isn't something forceful. It's more of a balancing act between credibility and connection that brings a quality of openness and curiosity to the situation. From there you can see what emerges and gently steer things by making clear and simple requests at the right moment (Cialdini, 2006; Rosenberg, 2015). You may be tempted to shout back at someone who is being aggressive. But it becomes much more obvious who is out of line by holding noble silence! Where dynamics get difficult is where two or more parties are focused on their own needs and ignoring those of others.

Being fluent in the language of needs helps you to not only be clear about what you want from people but also to understand what other people want on a deep level, even if they can't quite articulate it themselves. From there you can come up with creative ways to meet everyone's needs one way or another. Bringing awareness or mindfulness to interpersonal dynamics will be much more effective than trying tips and tricks to manipulate people.

Below are a few principles of communication from a framework called Non-Violent Communication (NVC). The core idea is that communication is much simpler if we see that most people's communication is a description of their strategy to meet perceived needs. By acknowledging this (in ourselves as well as others) we're less likely to manipulate people into trying to give us what we want and more likely to find collaborative solutions (Kashtan and Kashtan, nd). Some of the principles include:

- All human beings share the same needs.
- All actions are attempts to meet needs.
- Strategies we use to meet these needs may differ.
- Conflict occurs when we do not recognize needs or the existence of a range of strategies to meet them.
- Feelings are an indicator of needs being met or unmet.
- Human beings can facilitate meeting each other's needs through interdependent relationships.

USING NVC: TURN COMPLAINTS INTO REQUESTS
NVC strips down communication to its bare bones: observation, self-expression, request to meet a need. The principles are simple. Think about a conflict situation:

- Focus on what you observe and state the facts (not your interpretation of them).
- Acknowledge the impact on you (physically, practically and emotionally).
- Make a clear request as to what you'd like the person to do.

One way in which people get tripped up is by holding back or staying silent, because they're afraid the person will refuse or reject them. But we're all free agents. We can ask for anything we want and others have the right to say 'yes' or 'no'. We also have to trust that we can deal with the consequences of speaking what's true for us. The alternative is living in our mental trap.

Let's say you're trying to meet your need for contribution. A simple version of a non-violent statement is something like this:

> I've noticed that my request to take on more leadership has been delayed [Observation]. I feel frustrated about it [Impact on you]. I'd love the chance to contribute more to the team. Would you be willing to assign me to a project that gives me more responsibility, by the end of the month?

If the person doesn't meet your request and you're still unsatisfied, it may be time for a change of strategy. You only have three options in any situation: change the situation, change your attitude about the situation, or leave.

EMAILS

Emails have transformed the communication landscape. It's all too easy to fire off a damaging message in the heat of anger, or engage with stressful work messages outside working hours. However, emails can be turned into a tool for self-awareness by using the 'unsent email' approach. If you're dealing with a sensitive email that has triggered stressful thoughts or emotions, write an email response but sleep on it for at least 48 hours (long enough for your fight-flight-freeze response to settle). You can use the five questions of the HAPI process as a guide to processing it. After 48 hours check to see whether you feel the urge to send it. If the urge is still there, wait a little longer. When you're ready, use the NVC structure above.

MEETINGS

Too many meetings destroy team morale and drain energy. Meetings appear to have increased in length and frequency over the past 50 years to the point where executives spend an average of nearly 23 hours a week in them, up from less than 10 hours in the 1960s (Perlow *et al*, 2017). Ideas you may want to try or suggest for your next meeting:

- Start with an opening (mindful) pause so participants can settle down quietly and take a breath.
- Encourage vulnerability rather than status jostling. An example would be to invite people to: 1) share a success they are proud of followed by, 2) sharing one challenge they are struggling with.
- Listen for insight not opinion. Use your self-awareness to notice whether your thoughts are oriented towards agreement/

disagreement with what's being said in the meeting or whether you're tuning into your own 'aha' moments and sharing them.
• You may notice people default to a contrarian mode of conversation and use 'yes, but...' type sentences. A simple way to open up the conversation, keep it flowing and facilitate creative thinking is to invite people to use: 'yes, and...' so they can build on a previous statement rather than negate it entirely.

PRESENTATIONS

Depending on your professional context, presentations may incline towards heavily technical at one end or towards style-without-substance at the other. Like influence, the key to powerful presentations is balancing credibility and connection as you tell a story. It's important to share valuable information and ideas, but it's ineffective if your audience isn't interested. Fostering human connection through stories and humour, for example, can make all the difference. In the end, psychological safety – through connection and credibility – is essential if information is to be turned into action by teams.

Receive: patience and acknowledgement

The chapter so far has focused on what you can do to act on insights you have gleaned from your work to break free of the Success Trap. Eventually, when you've done everything you can do, there comes a time to let go and return to a more restful and receptive state. This requires patience as you wait to reap the fruit of the seeds you've sown. This waiting can be uncomfortable if you've been a high achiever, because you're stepping out of the active 'doer' mode. But you've got the tools to examine these uncomfortable states of mind. An additional tool is acknowledgement, which we talked about in Part Two. You acknowledge what you've done so far, your courage and your commitment, and celebrate it.

Staying free

Self-awareness is a tool, but it's also a way of living. If you're self-aware (mindful) all day, then your life becomes an opportunity for continuously breaking free of old traps. You have material to practise self-enquiry and self-mastery all day long: the colleague who was rude to you, the project that's stressing you, the decision to leave your job or not. Every single one of these issues is made up of the same basic components (thoughts and emotions). As you slow down and practise, your perspective shifts, possibilities multiply and your life transforms one way or another.

It would be wonderful to be permanently liberated; however, more often than not, we taste freedom and then backtrack – it's two steps forward, one step back and that's ok. Transformation is more like an upward spiral than a straight line. The final chapters will look at some of the finer points of living life outside the Success Trap and handling decision-making around the new possibilities available to you.

CHAPTER EIGHT

Turning uncertainty into opportunity

In Chapter 1 we looked at the VUCA (volatile, uncertain, complex and ambiguous) world of the 21st century. Today, the world offers many reasons to be anxious about the future. Not only is the pace of life faster, but most industries (and therefore jobs) are subject to unpredictable and rapid disruption due to the speed of technological development. Overnight, established industries from coal mining to printed news can find themselves challenged by new technology and leave their employees' futures uncertain. Since the 1960s, the threat of nuclear mass destruction has loomed large, and today we're increasingly aware of the damage we're doing to our ecosystem and the growing risk of extreme weather events. However, as we've explored in previous chapters, uncertainty doesn't have to be a problem.

In this chapter, we continue our journey outside the trap. While fear of uncertainty can barricade us in a safe life and make the world seem very small, narrow and repetitive (life inside the Success Trap), embracing uncertainty does the opposite: it connects us to a sense of vastness and possibility. By shifting our perspective, we can turn uncertainty into opportunity and find a sense of possibility and joy that helps us make the most of the cards that we are dealt. This is where we discover the full possibility of being human – outside the safety of the trap. As the saying goes: *A ship in harbour is safe, but that is not what ships are built for* (Shedd, 1928).

COMFORT ZONE BIAS

As a species, we seem to be rather risk (and effort) averse. Given a choice between enjoying a barbecue on the beach or climbing a mountain, most people would probably choose the former. Experiments investigating how we evaluate risk show that we prefer to avoid loss at all costs (even if there's a possibility of gain). Sure, we'll take a chance at winning, but not if it jeopardizes what's already in the bag (Tversky and Kahneman, 1991). It's been called a *status quo bias* (Kahneman *et al*, 1991) – we might also call it a *comfort zone bias*.

As an example, in one experiment, a group of people was offered a coin toss with the following instruction: 'I'm going to toss a coin, and if it's tails, you lose £10. How much would you have to win if it's heads in order for this gamble to be acceptable to you?' In other words, how much would you need to have a chance at winning before you're willing to lose £10?

What would you do? It turns out people want more than £20 before it is acceptable. They want to know that they might win double before they're willing to lose. This condition is unrelated to the actual amount of money at stake. The researchers found the same bias in very rich people (asking them about tossing a coin and losing £10,000 if it's tails). They'd need to feel they might win £20,000 before being willing to risk losing £10,000 (Richards, 2013). The comfort zone seems to be an engrained bias: given a choice, we'd rather stick to what we have than take a risk, unless there's a chance to win really big.

Three types of uncertainty

Contrary to popular perception, entrepreneurs are as loss averse as everyone else (Brown, 2014). The stereotype in the public imagination is of the audacious Richard Branson or Elon Musk who appear to gamble staggering amounts of money on a single idea or product. But it's not quite as it seems.

Note that loss aversion, risk taking and facing uncertainty are not entirely the same. You can still take a risk even if you are averse to loss or prefer your comfort zone. It would be more accurate to say that entrepreneurs (and people who take risks) make a deliberate, conscious choice to take a risk. They acknowledge the uncertainty and find innovative, creative ways to turn it into opportunity. They strategize to minimize losses while taking risks that can return large gains.

So, while uncertainty is a fact of life, the attitude or mindset we adopt in the face of uncertainty is what matters. It shapes our actions, identities and career paths. While most humans tend to avoid the possibility of loss (*loss aversion* or *comfort zone bias*), you can take a different approach. Let's look at three types of uncertainty. These are based on the work of economist Frank Knight (Sarasvathy, 2014).

Type 1: Risk (quantifiable and predictable)

You feel you know the probability of an outcome. For example, you might know that getting the job you want is a 50:50 chance, more or less, provided you do a reasonable job at the interview. This kind of situation can feel comfortable and perhaps a little boring to those who like a challenge because of its level of predictability.

Type 2: Ordinary uncertainty (quantifiable but not predictable)

You don't know the probability of an outcome but know it's possible. You may have found a dream job advert but have no idea what your chances are of getting it. There may be too many variables or unknowns. For example, you don't know how many candidates will be at the interview, you have no idea how you compare to them, or even whether your skills match up to what's needed. This is clearly a more challenging situation but also potentially exciting if you think of it as throwing your hat into the ring and seeing what happens. On the downside, it might feel as though you're on a wild goose chase if you keep applying for jobs without getting anywhere and have no idea why.

Type 3: True (Knightian) uncertainty (non-quantifiable, non-predictable)

You have no idea whether the outcome you have in mind is possible at all, let alone what your chances are. It may appear impossible, since no one has ever done it before, at least as far as you know. Perhaps the job that's perfect for you doesn't exist yet, and you would have to invent it yourself and create the structure for it. You might take it one small step at a time (which can feel like taking a stab in the dark), but each attempt gives you new information, new opportunities and new connections. It's the beginning of a creative cycle. With enough iterations, you may start to discern the probabilities more clearly or it might seem impossible right until it's done. Elon Musk famously said when his private rocket ship was finally launched, 17 years after he initiated the project (SpaceX): 'I always thought we would fail, so, this is all upside' (Clifford, 2019).

When you start out in your career, you might be operating in the context of the first two types of uncertainty. As you develop in experience, skills and connections, a time comes to break out of the Success Trap and look at creating the right opportunity. It doesn't mean you have to set up your own business, although that is of course an option; but you may find ways to develop while in employment with an organization, such as taking on more initiative, bringing innovative ideas and influencing others to enrol them in the idea to join you in a Creative Cycle.

Responding to uncertainty

There's often a very visceral, physical feeling that arises from the gut level when we step into the unknown. But you get used to it. This is the entrepreneurial mindset, which we'll explore in more detail in the next chapter. Dealing with uncertainty creatively and productively is arguably a core trait of the entrepreneurial mindset. However, while this trait is often associated with entrepreneurs, it's increasingly recognized as critical for 21st-century leadership and as a top soft skill for everyone working in an uncertain, VUCA world (Barton *et al*, 2012; Bennett and Lemoine, 2014).

What does dealing with uncertainty actually mean? Do entrepreneurs take unnecessary and dangerous risks for the fun of it? Are they adrenaline junkies of the business world? If that were the case, entrepreneurship would only attract the most heedless and reckless personalities. And yet, there are plenty of entrepreneurs who build their businesses slowly and steadily over decades, providing employment for others and creating products and services of value to society.

The key thing to remember is that life is inherently uncertain. Working in an organization can shelter us from this visceral experience of uncertainty, as we believe the organization will still be here tomorrow and we can count on it for a salary, a place to work, etc. But no one can truly predict what will happen next year, or even in the next moment. The ability to acknowledge this uncertainty while staying calm and creative is self-mastery and self-leadership that gives you the freedom to choose. As Kierkegaard (1844) said: *anxiety is the dizziness of freedom.*

RESPONDING TO UNCERTAINTY

Let's use the emotional cycle of change framework from Chapter 6 to understand how you tend to respond to uncertainty. This will help you see which strengths you can draw on and where you might need to do more work to step into the unknown and operate with more freedom and flow in the 21st century. Self-leadership – the ability to embrace the unknown and stay centred even if all others have lost themselves in fear – is the foundation of modern leadership.

How do you respond to uncertainty?

1 Uninformed/blind optimism (Yay! Change is awesome!)
   a. Advantage: Good ideas and enthusiasm.
   b. Disadvantage: Risk of not turning ideas into action, results and remuneration.
2 Informed pessimism (Oh, this is a little tricky and might take a while…)
   a. Advantage: Can see the pitfalls.
   b. Disadvantage: So self-critical that unlikely to step out of comfort zone or take action on ideas.
3 Valley of despair (*%$#! I have no idea what's going on!)
   a. Advantage: Can build resilience and high tolerance to risk with enough self-awareness.
   b. Disadvantage: Giving up early.
4 Informed optimism (ok, this could work out in an unexpected way. Let's see where the opportunities are.)
   a. Advantage: Right balance of ideas and positive action.
   b. Disadvantage: Can forget to bring people along or get support.

Now let's test your risk appetite and openness to experience. If you're ready for a new type of job, which approach do you take?

A   Wait until you really have to apply for a new job and apply for jobs that you are likely to get. Perhaps you mentally compute the odds of getting it (eg you find out how many other candidates there are and investigate their profiles). Perhaps you wait until the next round of applications to give you time to acquire a new qualification or gain more experience. You hate self-promotion and hope that someone will finally see the bright star that you are and give you the chance you deserve.

B   You use your intuition to guide you as to where to look for jobs and apply even if they don't seem like the logical match for your career profile as long as they sound interesting to you. You don't pay so much attention to the odds as much as to whether you're excited about the process. You build up all the skills you need as fast as you can and make new connections by asking for informational interviews. You're not shy about the talents and experience you bring and present them as a clear advantage for your potential new employer.

C   You don't care whether the job already exists; you are going to create it yourself, either within an organization or through your own business. You are always scanning your environment for exciting opportunities and coming up with big ideas that you test out and learn from until you hit the sweet spot – *Ikigai*! (See Chapter 7.)

Stepping into opportunity

The idea of stepping into the unknown isn't something that most people would want to engage in on a regular basis or find fun – after all our brain tries to avoid loss at all costs and the unknown entails a risk of loss – but as we can see, taking a risk and step-ping into the unknown can be the door to real freedom and fulfilment in life. It's the doorway out of the Success Trap.

It may be tempting to believe that there's a perfect job out there that will make you feel happy while paying you well. Perhaps you'll find the ideal role that challenges and supports you in just the right way... But in my experience, it doesn't usually land in your lap while you're hiding in your comfort zone.

CASE STUDY   The surgeon who embraced uncertainty

Athena, a talented surgeon, really wanted to reduce day-to-day clinical work and focus more on global health research and humanitarian work, possibly relocating her family to another country where she would provide care to communities that didn't have access to basic surgical care in her specialty. Her plan was to go the traditional academic route and complete a PhD. Her challenge was getting the funding for her dream research project. She was focused on this one goal and not getting very far despite many attempts.

Through the HAPI process in Chapter 6, we brought awareness to her patterns around uncertainty. She noticed a need to control and an attachment to the desired outcome. She also started to notice how this didn't help. As she gave herself permission to relax into her current situation, new opportunities started to appear: invitations to speak internationally and participate in philanthropic programmes. Her bosses couldn't help her enough and found ways to finance her role so she could remain on staff as things worked themselves out. Her status as successor to one of her mentors was cemented and her future in global health was all but certain by the end of a year. One day, while writing a funding application, Athena had an insight that it may be time to leave her clinical role and focus on her research and global health work. She noticed that she could still financially support herself and her family. This would give her complete freedom to do what she loved. Serendipitously, UNICEF contacted her to be part of one of their task forces in her area of interest, while up until then it had been impossible to connect with people in the organization! By embracing uncertainty, she unearthed a goldmine of opportunity. As a result of her courage and commitment, opportunities started to find her. She was in the flow.

The outcome you want in your career or life may not look exactly like you imagined or happen by the time you want it to. By letting go of the need to eradicate uncertainty, maintain safety and control outcomes, you can spot the opportunities available and enable a fulfilling outcome to unfold in its own time. It unfolds much faster than if you keep pushing. You may be pleasantly surprised by what unfolds, too. Often something much better will come along or you realize that it was staring you in the face. Stepping into the unknown creates a ripple of opportunities including the opportunity to have impact, the opportunity to do something meaningful and the opportunity to innovate. It's ultimately an opportunity to co-create experiences and things in collaboration with the people and circumstances around you.

The opportunity to have impact

Think of people you admire. They may not be perfect, but they probably inspire and encourage you. For me, these are usually people who have faced great challenges and turned them around. It reassures me to know that scientists and social activists who defied expectations of their times like Martin Luther King, Galileo, Gandhi, Malala Yousafzai, Mother Teresa all faced great uncertainty and embraced it as part of their path. The courage they tapped into led to new possibilities for the world.

The opportunity to do something meaningful

Simple actions can have great meaning. Think of Rosa Parks or Greta Thunberg. Plenty of people stay trapped in busy jobs jumping through meaningless hoops. But hopefully by now, you know that ticking boxes and jumping through hoops to land your dream job is unlikely to be the best strategy. By embracing the unknown, even small actions can turn into something meaningful if you're willing to take a stand for what you know to be true. You'll feel a sense of alignment with your deepest values, even if things get tough sometimes. Fear of visibility and fear of rejection are the biggest enemies to be aware of.

The opportunity to innovate

By embracing the unknown you're able to give more space to your own creativity and ability to think outside the box, as most entrepreneurs will tell you. These principles apply to both individuals and organizations. You can create the opportunity to innovate and lead. Innovation requires risk in the form of changing something (the product, services or the audience that made you or the organization so successful in the past). Organizations that failed to take a risk and innovate, like Kodak and Blockbuster, became obsolete because they stayed in their comfort zone and ended up exiting the market. It's called the Organizational Success Trap and results from a preference for business strategies that proved successful in the past over learning and experimentation (Askvik, 2002). You can see the parallels at the individual level and the High Achiever Paradox.

WHAT EMBRACING UNCERTAINTY DOES NOT LOOK LIKE

The opposite of embracing uncertainty is called intolerance of ambiguity. In 1949 a psychology professor at Berkeley, California, studied the relationship between tolerance to ambiguity and authoritarianism. Else Frenkel-Brunswik's work laid a foundation for understanding how our attitude to the uncertain, complex and unpredictable affects our decisions in life. Here are the nine primary characteristics that describe intolerance of ambiguity (Bochner, 1965):

1 need for certainty;

2 need to categorize and label things;

3 inability to allow good and bad traits to exist in the same person;

---

4   a white-black view of life;

5   a preference for familiar over unfamiliar;

6   rejection of the unusual or different;

7   resistance to reversal of a situation;

8   sticking to a single solution in an ambiguous situation;

9   premature action and closure.

Do you recognize any of these in yourself or others? If so, don't worry. We all carry these to some extent. They're attitudes underpinned by unhelpful beliefs that can be explored using the coaching tools we've been working with in this book (self-enquiry and self-mastery). An example is 'I need to know the answers now', as we looked at in Chapter 6. What would life be like if you let go of the belief: I need to know the answers before I step outside my comfort zone? What becomes possible without this belief?

It's probably best to see your tolerance to ambiguity as a fluid mindset rather than a new personality you have to acquire. Sometimes you feel confident and sometimes you don't. The good news is that confidence is not a requirement of action and you have tools to transform limiting beliefs so that you have more freedom to choose. A commitment to doing this work puts you at an advantage because 21st-century careers are complex and uncertain. If you can be patient with the ambiguous situations and complex information, you expand your opportunities for positive impact and meaning (Xu and Tracey, 2015).

Living from possibility: self-leadership in action

If you've given yourself permission to slow down (you can revisit Chapter 5 for tips and strategies), allowed your mind some space and made friends with the unknown using the HAPI process in Chapter 6, you'll inevitably have more capacity to generate great ideas around your next step towards a job, project or mission in life that feels more aligned with your values. You'll also have more energy to follow through with action. It may be as simple as taking a day off and organizing yourself, or going for a coffee with that person you met at a conference last month. The opportunities will multiply because you've created space for them and you're taking a step forward.

Recall the talented surgeon from the case study earlier in this chapter. As she let go of her attachment to how her global health work should look and where the funding should come from, she started to make new connections and enter new conversations. New opportunities started to appear serendipitously out of nowhere. This led to new collaborations and a restructuring of her work so that it included more global health work and less UK hospital work. She had more opportunities than she could handle at one point. The pressure to get to a destination started to lift and she started to enjoy the unfolding. She started to see the long game. Her positive energy and poise obviously helped to attract new opportunities. She transformed from a *problem solver* (how can I get funding and make this happen?) to an *opportunity embracer* (what's the next opportunity on my path?)

If you're not seeing new opportunities on your path, go back to Part Two and use some of the tools for creating space like the energy audit and the questions for self-enquiry to see if any limiting thoughts are running at the back of your mind. Most importantly, slow down and dig deeper – even if you think you've already done some work around a limiting belief. You'll be surprised at how deep limiting beliefs can run and what can come up as you explore your assumptions. Clients regularly say that they thought they knew what the problem was only to discover something different was holding them back.

If you're familiar with the foundations of self-enquiry, here are some more advanced practices and principles for life outside the Success Trap and living from possibility.

Expand your tolerance for joyful possibility

When was the last time you experienced a sense of adventure? Or played a game that was challenging and fun? This is what creating a new role or career for yourself can feel like from the perspective of joyful possibility. Often, people in the Success Trap feel they've lost a sense of adventure, spontaneity and fun that they remember from their teenage years or 20s. By the late 30s their responsibilities feel too great: kids, mortgage, etc. But being responsible doesn't mean you have to cut yourself (or your family) off from joyful possibility.

My parents left their home country in their early 40s and started over from scratch pretty much. It was one of the most uncertain times of my life but also one of the most exciting because of the new possibilities emerging. Seeing the dynamism, resourcefulness and resilience of my parents in facing challenges was enlivening. I had role models of courage in them and we were closer as a family, too. After all, happiness isn't just safety but the freedom to take action in alignment with what you know to be true and valuable to you. Many philosophers have argued this like Nobel Prize winner in Economics Amartya Sen (Sen, 2001) or even Aristotle who stated in his book *Nichomachean Ethics*: 'to be a good human being is to be a happy human being and happiness is an activity of the soul expressing virtue' (Dowling and Yap, 2012).

How can you start associating risk with joy again? Reintroducing play and spontaneity can work. Turning tasks into games is another trick. Psychologists call this *gamification*. Have you ever noticed how a game is no fun if it's too easy? By definition, a game requires obstacles and uncertainty. Pick a challenge for yourself and see if you can turn it into a game. Give yourself permission to feel the joy of fun and playfulness regardless of the outcome. Celebrate the fact that you played and let go of the need to win or the fear of losing.

As an example, if you fear rejection, a game my coach invited me to play is collecting NOs. Your only task is to make as many requests as possible (invitations to coffee, attendance at board meetings, or job applications) and celebrate the rejections. Why? Because they are not a reflection of your worth, they are a sign of your courage and willingness to live from possibility. They're also an indicator that you're taking action. As you can imagine rejection becomes less daunting as a result and opportunities you previously thought impossible can materialize. The 'yesses' inevitably follow the 'nos', as long as you don't give up. J.K. Rowling's *Harry Potter* was rejected by 12 publishers. The Beatles were told that guitar bands were over. You can use this game for anything from expanding your network and job interviews to dating. You may enjoy the book *Go for No! Yes is the destination, no is how you get there* (Fenton and Waltz, 2010).

Of course, a good game isn't a walk in the park. Plenty of challenges will come up including material from your mind (limiting beliefs around money, self-worth, capability, etc) as well as intense emotions around failure and rejection. You have the tools in Chapter 6. A good gauge of whether you should embrace a possibility – like applying for a job or resigning from one – is the way it feels on a subtle level. If it evokes something between fear and excitement (which have the same physiology but different stories overlaid), you're on the right track. Of course, always check against your inner wisdom and test the idea if you can, as described in the Creative Cycle.

A limiting belief is always an unquestioned one

As you step into the unknown, your limbic system (the emotional part of your brain that seeks pleasure and avoids pain) might become overexcited and you might enter the limbic hijack we talked about in Chapters 5 and 6. It may start flashing all sorts of old memories and unhelpful narratives at you to signal that danger lies ahead and that you should stay in your comfort zone. For example, if your *modus operandi* is to be constantly active, that is your comfort zone. The challenge for you is to slow down. The mind will start flashing all sorts of memories of when you didn't do your homework and there were terrible consequences or you were called 'lazy'.

A classic fear in high achievers is that if they stop, they'll never get going again. Another is the belief that they've been successful in the past because they've been constantly active, vigilant and anxious. In this case, your limiting beliefs about what it means to slow down and take time off are what's holding you back from embracing the situation with courage and wisdom and catalysing the next great thing in your life – it's the *High Achiever Paradox*. However, your limbic system is biased. It favours the comfort of the known, eg 'being constantly busy and stressed has worked for me in the past, so let's just carry on even if I'm exhausted, anxious and miserable'. Stepping outside your comfort zone isn't the limbic system's job, its job is survival based on old patterns. Exploring the unknown and new opportunities is the job of your prefrontal cortex but you can't hear what it's telling you if you're constantly busy and active.

This is why meditation and other mindfulness tools are so helpful. You can detect when you've gone from an open-minded, relaxed mode to a stressed one. You may also notice that the thoughts in your mind are multiplying and rather critical: 'this won't work', 'you're being silly', 'who do you think you are?', 'you're being lazy' etc. It's the imposter phenomenon – a cluster of beliefs and assumptions that essentially have one message: *you're not good enough*. It keeps you blind to your deeper potential and to new possibilities. Question these thoughts and notice a sense of openness – the beginner's mind. From here it's easier to notice new possibilities and take action.

The antidote to doubt is commitment

Sitting in the unknown does not entail being continuously racked with doubt. Sitting in the unknown can be a calmly enlivening experience as you give yourself permission to relax and allow for new ideas and insights to emerge without pressure or judgement, ie mindfully. An acknowledgement of being in the 'not-knowing' phase of the Creative Cycle or the messy middle of the emotional cycle of change is an immense relief if you're stepping out of your comfort zone and going through change. You can be committed to being at peace, exactly where you are even if you have no idea where you are. When I've felt completely overwhelmed with uncertainty and committed to being in that moment, I've felt a weight lift off my shoulders and I often find myself just carrying on with what I was doing before, taking one step at a time.

If you're struggling to break out of doubt during a period of change or preparation for change, here are a few ideas to play with:

- Commit to not knowing by saying: I'm committed to not knowing the answers right now and I'm open to suggestions.
- Commit to doing what's in front of you (whether it's organizing your papers or chairing that meeting).
- Commit to a small step: email someone for an informational interview (to learn about their industry or job); arrange a day secondment to an organization you're interested in; or go to a gallery or natural setting and get inspired.
- Commit to investigating any stressful thoughts using self-enquiry and the HAPI process.
- Commit to helping someone else with the same problem(s) you're grappling with and watch the insights drop as you listen (no fixing or rescuing, just listening and empathizing).

The risk with the unknown is that you get sucked into anxious thoughts about *what if?* Committing to the unknown and to any creative action that cultivates openness, connection and curiosity is far more likely to help you break out of fear and have an 'aha moment' than repetitive, anxious thinking.

If in doubt, up your self-care

If you're a high achiever (whether you're of the imposter or rescuer variety), your tendency is to be hard on yourself for not knowing the answer. From now on, I invite you to err on the side of self-care. It is much more effective to gather your resources when facing the messy middle than to push yourself through self-criticism or unfocused, busy activity. Being tired, over-whelmed and isolated can put you firmly in limbic hijack and make things look much worse.

Give yourself permission to let go of expectations

Notwithstanding the fear of rejection and need for belonging described earlier, breaking out of the Success Trap for good requires that you become the author of your life going forward. Are you willing to go against the grain to create a career and life that feel more aligned? Are you able to self-lead and know that the locus of decision-making is firmly rooted within yourself and not in external sources of authority? You may think you're free of external influence but may be surprised if you look more care-fully at what's holding you back. By questioning limiting beliefs and narratives that come up, you free yourself to write a fresh new story moment to moment – you become self-authoring in the best sense. At this point, a new identity – as entrepreneur, artist, writer, educator, etc – can emerge. It's a new hat that you can put on and take off as needed. You can take an old identity along with you, not as a trap but as a resource.

Remember what you're willing to fail for

In the toughest moments of change, when the uncertainty is the greatest, it will help to remember your motivation for crossing this messy middle in the first place: what you're willing to fail for. This is where your deeper sense of who you are (including your purpose, mission, values or what Simon Sinek (2019) calls your 'why?') can come to your aid to bolster you. It may be your family, or a loved one or a cause beyond yourself. This is about remembering the bigger things that really matter to you, things that you would put everything on the line for.

Don't ask how you can find a job that will make you feel good and pay well, ask what you are willing to do – even if it's from a cardboard box. Shallow success is doing something that makes you feel hollow on the inside but looks good on the outside. Freedom and true happiness are following the wisdom and inspiration of your own inner genius even if it feels tough at times.

Action trumps perfection: experiment and learn

Have you had an insight but are procrastinating on taking action? Can you see a new opportunity but are afraid to try it out? Are you striving to be the perfect candidate before applying for a job you're interested in? If in doubt, take a small step forward and see what feedback you get. You might change perspective and gain sudden clarity. Perhaps you'll realize it definitely isn't the right job for you but you're glad you went to the interview because you made new connections. You experiment and learn and grow your circle of connection. There's no such thing as failure: it's all learning.

Go for the impossible!

The great thing about being willing to embrace uncertainty and face the unknown is that things that seemed impossible can start to materialize. An opportunity finally unlocks, you go to a meeting and the person you've been trying to contact is there. As you stay in the process, serendipity comes to your aid. Being less attached to outcomes also means you're able to enjoy the process. This gives you more energy to stay engaged with the process creating a virtuous cycle of change until the cycle feels complete. You might have a vision of raising a million dollars to help stop human trafficking or to get a thousand girls in sub-Saharan Africa through school. It doesn't matter what it is exactly, it's whether it moves you to take a step. Once you take a step, the next one reveals itself.

Work culture and leadership expert Simon Sinek's vision is a world where people wake up inspired, feel safe and valued at work and come home feeling fulfilled. He calls it the infinite game because this may not materialize within his lifetime (Sinek, 2019). He just sees himself as playing a part in the bigger symphony of life. For you it might be a world free of war, cancer or mental illness. You're not in competition with anyone, you're simply doing your part. We'll revisit this idea in Chapter 10.

Playing a big game doesn't mean you neglect your own needs and safety. I highly recommend making a sober assessment of your material and financial needs and ensuring they are covered one way or another. But the difference between a life in the Success Trap and a life outside it is that your material needs are a foundation rather than the goal. It also means your material needs are kept finite while your ability to engage with the opportunities around you becomes infinite.

Live in the learning zone

If you've ever tried something new, you'll know exactly how it feels to step into the unknown. It's that feeling when someone says 'jump' and you're not sure if it's safe, but you've seen others do it and they're safe on the other side and glowing with pride of accomplishment. You feel a bit of a knot in your stomach and the exhilaration of taking the leap. Whether this is before a bungee jump, sending an email asking for a pay rise, speaking up in a meeting or even sending your resignation letter, the physiology is the same.

The secret to not burning out or losing yourself in a maze of expectations is to remain self-aware. Through self-awareness and curiosity you can ask yourself the right questions and continuously learn and unlearn to adjust your mindset. Sure, you might be thrown off balance. But you know you can handle it. Any fear or stress can be examined through self-enquiry and dissolved through self-mastery.

The learning zone is somewhere between the comfort zone of automatic habits and old expectations, and the danger zone where your survival instincts are out of control leading you to panic or freeze. In the learning zone, you're gently and consistently taking steps, you walk the uncertain world we live in with a clear mind that discerns genuine opportunities from hyped up threats and act with wisdom.

In the next two chapters, we'll look at the entrepreneurial mindset in more detail and how to apply it to your career, and how we create a work culture where people have more freedom to contribute authentically.

CHAPTER NINE

From the employee-expert mindset to the entrepreneur-leader mindset

We live in an ideal era to start a business. The internet has democratized access to information and also to the opportunities to share a message, product or a service on an unprecedented scale with minimal investment (Priestley, 2013). The overheads for starting a business are potentially negligible, especially because you don't have to invest in physical premises, necessarily. With the availability of micro-entrepreneur platforms, free or near-free services on the cloud, and crowdfunding options, the material barriers to starting a new business are nearly negligible. The statistical trends suggest that Generation Z (the successors to Millennials) are eager to take the leap into entrepreneurship. They are more concerned with the stigma of not having tried to set up a business by the time they are 30, than with having tried to do so and failed (Koulopoulos, 2015).

While business ownership is not for everyone, being entrepreneurial is increasingly an advantage, and it doesn't have to be synonymous with starting a business. Your entrepreneurial spirit can manifest while you work within an organization through taking initiative, generating novel ideas and turning uncertainty into opportunity. It can also manifest in the way you navigate your career by creating opportunities and roles that work for you and contribute to your organization and society.

One thing I hope is clear from this book is that you don't have to give up your autonomy, compromise on important values or struggle alone to experience fulfilment in your work or career. On the contrary. What you want is often closer than you think, just behind a wall of fear. The key is to bring awareness to perceived obstacles, question old ways of being and thinking that create fear and confusion, and tap into your inner genius to guide you. You've done the heavy lifting in Part Two. Now, you can proactively integrate new insights and creative ideas into your way of working and leading – an entrepreneurial mindset.

The entrepreneur's capacity to innovate, scale and operate with more autonomy requires a tolerance for uncertainty. In the last chapter, we looked at the different types of uncertainty and how the entrepreneurs manage the loss aversion that we all experience. But what is the core trait of entrepreneurship? Can we learn it and apply it in traditional careers? Is entrepreneurialism about making money? Or is it the future of work culture? This chapter explores the entrepreneur mindset. We'll explore how it differs from the employee mindset, how it can help professionals to move from technical expert to leader, and ways you can develop your own entrepreneurialism and apply it to your career and mission in life.

From employee to entrepreneur

It's difficult to overestimate the impact of a shift in mindset in going from employee to entrepreneur (you have the tools in Part Two). As an employee, you may well find it acceptable to do something you don't love just for the salary and lifestyle. You normally have a schedule to follow that gives you structure. You're usually given some form of responsibility as well as tasks and goals to work towards. You have readily available opportunities to meet people every day, just by turning up to work. You might even have the chance to keep learning and developing through corporate training, peer-support or mentoring.

As an entrepreneur none of these is a given. The loneliness, lack of structure, absence of guidance and high uncertainty are a daily experience and can be paralysing. If you're not prepared or don't have sources of support to get you through, it's all too likely that you'll hit a wall and give up. (That's why it's often easier to have side-hustles or build a business slowly while paying the bills with a day-job than to take a leap into running your own business.) So leaping from employee to entrepreneur can be quite a shock to the system. Start-up statistics suggest that the most common reason that people start a business is being ready to be their own boss, followed by wanting to pursue a passion (Mansfield, 2019). If you're ready, then missing the jump off point may lead to frustration and disillusionment.

You may be ready for an employee-to-entrepreneur mindset shift if you're experiencing some of the following:

- You've had great success and feel there's something bigger or more fulfilling to step into.
- You feel frustrated in the absence of autonomy and/or creative freedom.
- You have a lot of ideas for projects, programmes, initiatives or even a business but you're not sure where to start or how to take the next step.
- You've spent enough time thinking about the next step or doing research about it. You've even consulted trusted sources about it and feel you can take an informed risk.

- You're aware of the uncertainty in your industry or job market and don't want to sit around waiting for someone else to decide your future.
- Your personal life or relationships are feeling the strain of indecision about what to do next.

Most tellingly, you're feeling a healthy mix of excitement and fear at the thought of taking the leap.

What makes an entrepreneur?

The term 'entrepreneur' covers a wide range of people and their ventures, from the 20-something venture capital-backed tech innovator to the 50-something solo consultant. Some scholars of capitalism have described entrepreneurs as those who like to ride the wave of change and engage in what's called 'creative destruction' (Schumpeter, 1942). Think of the Creative Cycle and how it goes through all the stages of innovation from the quiet phase required to let go of the old to make space for the new, to the testing and implementation of a new idea. An entrepreneur can navigate the whole cycle and make it the core of their job description: good at embracing uncertainty and the Creative Cycle described in Chapter 6.

One trait that appears consistently in those with an entrepreneurial orientation and less so in those who work as managers is *openness to experience*. 'Openness to experience' is one of the big five personality traits in psychology. It is defined as a love of being in the moment and learning from situations that are not necessarily associated with achievement. In contrast, people who are 'intellectually curious' have a love for academic knowledge, intellectual pursuits and abstract ideas. But the latter don't learn as well in complex, real life situations as those who are open to experience (von Stumm, 2018).

Alongside openness to experience, other traits that appear pretty consistent among entrepreneurs include (Kerr *et al*, 2017):

- Self-efficacy (being proactive) particularly in relation to risk-taking, marketing, management and financial control.
- Innovativeness (responding creatively to novel situations).
- Internal locus of control (believe that their own decisions control their lives rather than chance, fate, or environmental factors outside their control that they cannot influence.
- Need for achievement (have a desire for significant accomplishment, mastering of skills and attaining challenging goals).

Three types of entrepreneur

As mentioned, being entrepreneurial or developing an entrepreneur mindset doesn't have to imply that you must set up your own business. It can mean that you develop new ideas or projects and take on a greater role in leading business development, strategy or innovation in your organization. In the widest sense possible, being entrepreneurial means that you're open to whatever life throws at you, manage the discomfort (through self-enquiry and self-mastery, for example) and are prepared to turn uncertainty into opportunity to create something. Here are three types of entrepreneur you can choose from (Suárez-Álvarez and Pedrosa, 2016):

- **The classic entrepreneur** (extra-entrepreneur): sets up a new business as a vehicle for bringing a new product or service to the marketplace.
- **The organizational entrepreneur** (intra-entrepreneur or intra-preneur): innovates within an organization or company contributing to a pre-existing business strategy.
- **The personal entrepreneur:** skilled at taking initiative and handling uncertainty including stressors like unemployment or career changes.

The latter also includes those who work for social impact or human development such as the community organizer who innovates in mobilizing common resources to create social value; the activist who comes up with a new perspective and solution to an issue; and the researcher who proposes a novel theory or technique.

BUSINESS AND CAREERS ARE DYNAMIC, NOT FIXED

You've probably heard the expression: climbing the career ladder. It conveys the sense that there is a destination to get to by following a track. In a way, there is. Usually, there's only one CEO in a company, one Prime Minister, one head of operations. But these roles represent the same thing: power. If you're reading this book, the chances are you're not driven by a desire for power. I imagine you're more interested in doing something meaningful and living happily and peacefully. You may also want to experience connection, autonomy (freedom from the Success Trap!) and an outlet for your creativity – a sense of life lived and potential fulfilled.

If that is the case, you can relax. You don't have to aim for a particular role or job to feel successful. Gone are the days of the career for life, anyway. So there's no single track for success. You can release your entrepreneurial spirit and navigate the beautiful geometry of the career that's right for you. You might notice that when you work on one part of it, the rest of the structure changes. A new formation emerges with a new set of possibilities, opportunities and challenges. Then you use your skills and abilities to make the next inspired move. You may not be able to see the whole structure while you're building it. You create it as you go along making the most of circumstances, however uncertain they feel in the moment. You build the plane as you fly.

Navigating your career like an entrepreneur

If you've done the exercise in Chapter 8 on how you respond to uncertainty, you'll have an idea of what type of entrepreneur mindset you want to adopt.

- **If you identify mostly with (A)**: You may be more suited to being a *personal entrepreneur* and holding a salaried role but with enough autonomy and opportunity to innovate. Start connecting to what really matters to you, and make sure your career/job matches your values as much as possible. If you're not happy in your current role, take a step back and apply the principles in this book to help you see the bigger picture and spot opportunities. Do more of what energizes you or try something new on a regular basis, eg volunteering or contributing to a project you care about. Grow a community of likeminded people and mentors who will support you and match you up with the right opportunities. Make sure you nurture your network and give back to it.

- **If you identify mostly with (B)**: You may be suited to being an entrepreneur and leader in your field within an organization as an *intrapreneur*. Get familiar with your transferable strengths and your zone of genius. Learn to describe them to others (including in presentations and interviews) using examples and real stories of how they work. Develop leadership skills including influence, conflict resolution, speaking and delegation. Think about what your long-term contribution could be and make space to nurture it. If you have an office job, could you propose a new project, product or service that would add value to your clients or community? Could you start a business or Foundation on the side? Address any fear of visibility and tap into your network to help you refine your ideas. Start to share these as part of a wider conversation and think about collecting your best ideas.

- **If you identify mostly with (C)**: You may be suited to being a *classic entrepreneur* and running your own business. You're probably one of the 10 per cent who thrive under uncertain conditions and have an entrepreneurial spirit. Make sure you take action to implement your ideas or partner up with people who can help. Keep cultivating a healthy mindset and handling the four entrepreneur demons around uncertainty, structure, guidance and isolation (see below). If you're pitching for investment then handle fear of rejection and failure and hone your communication and leadership skills to be able to mobilize resources and get people on board.

In all three cases, you can learn to thrive under the uncertain conditions in the VUCA world.

Finding your passion

I often hear people saying that they want to find their passion and that once they do, they'll know what steps to take to get out of a job or career they don't like. This may be true on one level: if you discover a new passion, there may well be a job that matches up to it. For example, if you love writing, teaching or gardening, there are pre-existing jobs in the economy to accommodate this. However, objections will soon come into play. After all, living from selling books is not usually lucrative, teaching in deprived schools can be challenging, gardening may require you to start again from scratch and learn business skills. So knowing your passion is not enough.

It's also true that holding a strong vision helps to move forward and overcome obstacles. Or at least, that's what conventional wisdom says about leadership and entrepreneurship. Knowing what you're working towards helps you focus, and focusing on things that you care about energizes you.

Professionals in the knowledge economy are handicapped by their need to claim expert status and appear knowledgeable. It's anathema to the beginner's mind discussed in Chapter 6 that serves transformation, mindfulness and entrepreneurship. An entrepreneur going through a Creative Cycle is required to embrace uncertainty and the possibility of failure as a good thing, two things an employed professional normally tries to avoid at all costs. While technical expertise has a place in solving problems and providing services, if an identity is built around it one can find oneself trapped in a job and completely blind to one's transferable skills and innate genius.

Individuals who acknowledge the importance of embracing uncertainty as a key skill or trait are more likely to thrive in the 21st century. Those who also apply it to the inevitable ambiguity of their own career decision-making are less likely to have distorted career beliefs and get stuck (Xu and Tracey, 2015). Individuals who don't, are likely to start chasing elusive concepts like passion, purpose, values, etc hoping that identifying these will remove the inherent uncertainty and discomfort of stepping outside the prescribed identities and roles they've grown accustomed to (their comfort zone). It won't.

Passion can't protect you from uncertainty

Finding one's passion is no guarantee against duress and uncertainty, or ensures you'll be wealthy and happy for the rest of your life. History is replete with examples of people who transformed the world and who faced what we would call 'tough career decisions'. They had the equivalent of the mortgage, bills, school fees to worry about and more: like the next invasion or outbreak of the plague. Did you know that Galileo started off as a medical student? He originally wanted to become a priest, but his father encouraged him to enrol in medical school as a more lucrative outlet for his altruistic motives. He discovered a passion for mathematics and the natural sciences while at medical school and nurtured a love for art and music. But his father wanted him to focus on medicine as a more secure profession that paid better. The family was indebted, as two of his siblings had died leaving a heavy burden on the family.

Galileo took it one step at a time and changed track to become one of the greatest scientists with a detour as an arts teacher along the way! He defied the most powerful institutions of his day and our understanding of the universe changed. We became a more enlightened society because people like him were willing to go against the grain and go beyond what seemed safe and certain, radically challenging societal expectations. He faced incredible duress for challenging old ideas and narrowly escaped torture and execution. For his defence of heliocentrism, he spent almost a decade under house arrest until his death. He faced uncertainty and the unknown continuously.

Passion also has a dark side. Higher rates of burnout occur among entrepreneurs who can't switch off from their work. It is hard to switch off if you don't have a fixed schedule, lack cues to stop working, or feel anxious about not making next month's payroll for your employees. However, entrepreneurs who are too passionate or 'obsessively passionate' appear to be at higher risk of a breakdown (De Mol *et al*, 2018).

Passion is a by-product of risk

Games aren't fun if they're too easy. That's why the predilection for comfort (comfort zone bias/loss aversion) that keeps us in the Success Trap also strips our life of the joy and exhilaration we experienced as children. It's also why flirting and seduction fall flat if the outcome is already known. People worry about not knowing their passion and feel that not having one is what's holding them back in life or keeping them bored. The truth is that passion is the result of being willing to take a risk.

In my experience working with high achievers, the key to breaking out of the Success Trap isn't passion or vision but the ability to tolerate uncertainty – what some psychologists call tolerance of ambiguity and openness to experience – the core trait of the entrepreneur mindset. The ability to sit in the 'not knowing' phase of change, the Creative Cycle, the messy middle or the 'space between stories' restores a powerful sense of agency and transforms fear into excitement.

For more fulfilment and less drudgery in work, reverse the causal relationship between passion and risk: *don't try to find your passion to take a risk in your career, take a risk and let your passion find you.* Galileo isn't remembered for 'following his passion'. He's remembered for risking everything to challenge dogma. He questioned the beliefs held by the most powerful institutions of his day. He probably had no idea what would happen to him on many occasions. But it didn't stop him.

Many of my clients stumble upon their passion as they take a leap and sit in 'not knowing' for a while. They question the expectations and beliefs handed down to them and open up to new perspectives. As a result, new possibilities come into view. This puts them on a new trajectory. No passion or confidence required. Just a willingness to remain open despite the discomfort and take one small change at a time.

CASE STUDY Hermione

Hermione, a creative marketing and business consultant, had worked with big brands and decided to take a leap out of a job that didn't fit anymore. She spent a few weeks truly taking care of herself and enjoying the natural landscape near her home while releasing any old expectations. Within three months she'd set up her own consultancy helping small businesses to think outside the box and serve their clients better. Her services were wonderfully innovative and even included a walking consultation – after all why should meetings be confined to seated conversation?

No one can predict what will happen when someone embraces the unknown. Often, they give attention to areas of their life that they'd neglected for a while and find that repairing their relationships and improving their health are a priority. They might leave their job and try something different, get the promotion they'd wanted, or take the entrepreneurial route to start or grow a high value business that plays to their strengths. If they embrace the journey, they find themselves living with more exhilaration, less fear and deeper fulfilment.

Your past successes are not your destiny, they're your capital

If you're a high achiever, chances are you're very good at what you do. You're probably good at several things – you have many zones of competence and a number of zones of excellence, as Gay Hendricks calls them (Hendricks, 2009). This can create the dilemma of choice. How do you pick from the many things you're good at? Perhaps your analytical, problem-solving skills are rivalled by your talent for managing stakeholders and facilitating productive meetings. Perhaps you can bake the perfect soufflé or ski like a champion.

If you try to make decisions based on your strengths, you can get very confused. Your strengths may be the result of rigorous training and a long history of practice as well as the societal preferences that were impressed upon you as to what is useful and lucrative. While it's helpful to take your strengths into account, remember *Ikigai* – the sweet spot at the intersection of what you love, what you're good at, what the world needs and what the world can pay you for.

What I've noticed is that high performers who exit the Success Trap create a rich tapestry made of pre-existing skills and strengths as well as unacknowledged talents and forgotten sources of inspiration that they start to cultivate more consciously like an ability for deep listening. They interweave old parts of themselves with undiscovered or forgotten parts of themselves. Over time, they connect with and embody their zone of genius. One person might be incredible at providing deep insights into the complexity and possibilities of a zero-carbon economy. Another might have a second-to-none ability to read people and manage global teams. Yet another might remain eerily calm in a crisis and able to perform life-saving surgery in a war zone. If they embrace their voice as thought leaders, they cultivate skills for sharing ideas through writing and speaking to translate complex ideas into simple ones that increase access to their deep insights.

And it's never too late.

Anna Moses (also known as Grandma Moses) was a house-wife with a knack for embroidery. When her arthritis got in the way, she picked up a paintbrush and began painting rural land-scapes at the tender age of 76 years. She produced more than 1,500 paintings over the ensuing three decades. Having sold her early paintings for US $4, her fame grew and so did the price of her paintings; one of her paintings sold for US $1.2 million in 2006. She lived to 101 and was named young woman of the year at age 88!

While this example is dramatic, it illustrates one principle: *your future is not determined by your past*. Letting go of your past strengths and successes can help you soar to new, unpredictable heights of success and creative joys. It's a principle I had to learn myself in making career decisions. For example, I had undergone some of the most extensive and elite training possible as a doctor, but I realized one day that being good at something like research doesn't mean it's the career for you. However, I could weave research into anything I did and improve its quality and validity.

In summary, don't be guided by your zone(s) of competence or even your zone(s) of excellence to make career decisions. Use them as capital to invest in your next step and reveal your zone of genius. Even if you discover it at 76 years like Grandma Moses, it will have been worth it. With time and a bit of courage following the principles in this book, you'll find you were on your path all along.

The independent professional's four demons

The body of research on the fears that entrepreneurs face tends to focus on fear of failure (Cacciotti and Hayton, 2015). However, other subtypes of fear exist for people who choose to be their own boss. Fear is a rich source of insight if we're willing to identify and question the story behind it. It can also become a powerful source of motivation if you transform it into excitement and channel the energy into the Creative Cycle. In the few years I've been a business owner and worked independently, I've noticed four types of fear that show up on a regular basis and elicit nods of agreement from fellow business owners:

1 lack of structure (I don't know where to start);
2 isolation;
3 financial uncertainty;
4 lack of guidance (I don't know what to do).

Let's look at an example of how they play out. You may be a brilliant big picture thinker, problem solver and connector like Xena who worked with intergovernmental organizations then decided to take the leap and set up her own business (see Chapter 3). She realized what her zone of genius was almost immediately: helping people see through complexity. As she knuckled down to deliver, she started to notice that she didn't always know where to begin her day or how to organize it. Working from home meant that she couldn't just turn to the person sitting next to her and chat about it or ask a boss. She started to feel isolated and anxious. She also noticed that she didn't always know where the next client would come from and the uncertainty and isolation were compounding each other.

It's tempting at this point to start looking backwards. You're in the messy middle of change. Expectations from the old world are still active, while the new world isn't quite established. But she wasn't willing to give up. She slowed down and worked on the narratives and beliefs that were running through her mind. They included 'I am alone' and 'I don't know what to do'. By exploring these and challenging the truth of them, she started to remember how great she was at connecting and creating relationships. It was challenging when the instruction was to take a break or take a day off. But she eventually started to settle into a new rhythm of work and saw how great it was to be able to make a living from her business working with great clients who appreciated her.

She realized that she was still putting a lot of pressure on herself and what she really wanted was more room for creative writing, family and travel. We discussed practical solutions for each of the challenges. But if we'd gone straight to trying to fix the fears rather than exploring them and discovering what was really needed, we may have missed the insights the fears had to offer. Slowing down, making room for creativity and implementing small modifications to her day did the trick.

DELTA IS FOR DREAM

Summarizing the traits of an entrepreneurial mindset, we can list these as:

1 Dream big.

2 Embrace uncertainty.

3 Leap (one step at a time).

4 Test and learn.

5 Appreciate yourself and watch out for your inner critic.

Daily practices for the entrepreneurially minded include:

1 Tune in to yourself every day (me-time/self-care) for self-mastery.

2 Remember the bigger picture that inspires you.

3 Challenge yourself in a small way every day (get out of your comfort zone).

4 Turn difficult experiences into insights (learning) – use self-enquiry.

5 Optimism: allow your dreamer to imagine possibilities and tell the better story.

6 Get support: 'heroes aren't scalable!'

7 Keep it simple.

Starting capital

When thinking of starting a business, people typically think of money as the main resource needed. Indeed, the famous young Silicon Valley tech entrepreneurs like Steve Jobs or Mark Zuckerberg who made entrepreneurship glamorous needed money for their ventures. They needed big investments to scale their businesses beyond the garage and university campus they respectively started in.

But as we saw earlier, entrepreneurs come in many shapes and sizes. The 20-something venture capital-backed demographic of entrepreneur is different from the mid-career professional with years of experience. If you're in the latter group, you have a wealth of career capital to draw on, including if you're converting to a different career.

Evidence suggests that the most successful entrepreneurs (those who have spent several years on this path and have taken at least one company public) use both external and internal resources at their disposal as capital (Read *et al*, 2016). External capital includes the investment, physical assets and so on. Internal capital includes your transferable skills, your mindset and your commitment to do what it takes (including the work we've talked about in this book). It's thought that the ability to identify opportunities and commit to them is the single most important factor for entrepreneurial success (Erikson, 2002).

There are only three core business activities: sales, marketing and delivery within a respectful relationship with your clients. As a professional, you'll have multiple skills that can be transferred to each of these areas of business alongside any specialist knowledge. For example, if you have management and planning skills, you'll be able to establish priorities, use time and resources wisely, and get things done. Your intellectual and creative abilities will help you analyse data, research options and design strategies that develop your business. Table 9.1 is a list of transferable skills to remind you of what you can do (Shirey, 2009).

TABLE 9.1 Transferable skills

Writing	Interpersonal skills	Negotiation skills
Analysing	Team player	Public speaking
Research	Event coordination	Working well under
Teaching and training	Cultural competence	pressure
Decision-making	Creative thinking	Organizing/project
Planning	Advocacy	management
Forecasting	Foreign language	Teaching and training
Coding	skills	Time management
Computer literacy and	Delegating	Conflict resolution
special software	Flexibility and	Influencing
literacy	adaptability	Proofreading and
	Problem-solving skills	editing

ENERGY IS A PRECIOUS ASSET

Your energy is an important aspect of your capital. If you have a boss, you are driven by their expectations to work hard and deliver. When you are your own boss, you have to motivate yourself in other ways. You also have to be judicious in your use of energy and regulate your energy levels yourself. Burning out is a huge liability to your business, so care is required. As we saw earlier, being too passionate is a risk factor for entrepreneurial burnout (De Mol and Ho, 2018).

There'll be days when you're bursting with enthusiasm. Others you'll be unsure why you should get out of bed. It's important to maintain your energy levels within a safe window that is sustainable for the long term, so self-mastery is important here. Honouring your rhythm of Creative Cycles (including periods of quiet) is part of this. If you need to make arrangements or take a part-time job to reduce financial pressure, then do so. It will make your entrepreneurial endeavours sustainable in the long term. It's a marathon not a sprint.

Scaling vs company of one

There's a belief among entrepreneurs that a product or service has to be scalable. Scaling means that you expand the distribution and sales of your product. It requires systematic changes to how the business is run as well as hiring and managing new people and potentially gaining new investment to support expansion. This can be great fun and extremely satisfying. It's also a source of increased complexity, uncertainty and relationship stress from dealing with more people and processes.

When I started out, I was asked if I had plans to train other coaches and have them do the coaching while I focused on business development. I was advised by an experienced entrepreneur that working to sell a coaching franchise would be more lucrative than the sole-practitioner-based business model I was following. While this might be true, it's not necessarily the right model for me. So many different factors are at play. Fortunately, I worked with a coach who did not follow the scaling model and was very successful. He had tried to scale using conventional advice and realized it didn't work for him.

If you're not keen on large and complex processes or dealing with a lot of people, perhaps you're more introverted, but are drawn to the entrepreneurial way of life, you can still succeed. In his book a *Company of One*, Paul Jarvis (2019) suggests that the key to more fulfilling entrepreneurship is not to create and scale something into a massive corporation, but rather to work for yourself, determine your own hours and become a sustainable solo operation that gives you both freedom and remuneration.

The many faces of the entrepreneur

So having an entrepreneurial orientation can take many forms. While there are no guarantees, if you're willing to do the work, build on pre-existing career capital and embrace the opportunities amid uncertainty, you can thrive. Using the tools and principles in this book you can overcome the common demons of the entrepreneur mindset around uncertainty, isolation, structure and the need for an external source of authority to tell you what to do. You can contribute to the future of work in an uncertain world both directly through the services you offer as well as by the example you set for others. In the next chapter, we'll look at what a healthy work culture might look like as we bring an entrepreneurial mindset and greater psychological safety to our collaborations.

CHAPTER TEN

Work cultures that liberate

Perhaps when you picked up this book, you were wondering about your career direction. Maybe you felt you were caught in a Success Trap and were ready for a radical change. Now, you may have reconnected with a deeper aspect of you, your 'inner genius'. Hopefully, you'll know that wherever you are is the perfect place to break free of any perceived limitations and allow your natural inspiration to guide you.

But what happens when you're out there in the big wide world? When work pressures, frustrating situations and difficult colleagues come rushing into view again? And what about wider society? If everyone is rushing around, competing and elbowing each other out of the way, won't you get left behind by relaxing? What would it be like if our work culture encouraged a slower pace, deeper trust and more freedom?

Below are a few final insights to consider on how we can make the world of work a realm for the inner genius (creativity is the most sought after skill after all) rather than a place of drudgery to meet material needs, at an individual and collective level. What might a world of compassionate ruthlessness look like, where we enable creative thinking through psychological safety and uproot old, binding assumptions ruthlessly? If we each started to take greater responsibility for our automatic patterns of thinking and behaving, perhaps a tipping point might be reached in the not so distant future. Then a work culture that enables more freedom, creativity and wellbeing might flourish.

Wouldn't it be great to have a world where going to work isn't a threat or place of drudgery? Is it too much to hope that *people wake up inspired and excited to work, feel safe and valued at work, and return home fulfilled*? I may be an optimist but I know I'm not the only one (Sinek, 2019).

Culture, bias and trust in the workplace

As someone who has spent 24 years in formal education between two very different countries and experienced a range of work cultures, I believe that no work is more important than questioning the thoughts, beliefs and cultural myths that populate our survival focused brain. By staying open to experience and cultivating curiosity, we can ward off the ills of rigid, habitual thinking and toxic narratives that we've internalized. By questioning them, we can stay sane and connected to our zone of genius. Otherwise, our capacity to weave beliefs into myths, culture and dogma will continue to trap us in unsatisfying situations.

A large body of work exists around perception and bias in psychology, philosophy, neuroscience and the relatively new field of behavioural economics (Etzioni, 2011). As a scientist, bias is a bane. It's impossible to produce high quality research and derive accurate conclusions from experiments if bias is present, so most research methods are designed to eliminate bias. Is it possible for us to be a little more scientific about our opinions and emotions in the workplace? If our organizations are magical laboratories of sorts, where we're trying to create and provide products and services that are valuable to people, shouldn't we apply scientific principles to our own thinking?

Confirmation bias is possibly the most insidious form, since it creates a double blind-spot: not only do we have a bias, we'll also ignore information that might help us question it. It's not just that we don't have the full picture, we'll keep picking up information that reinforces our own view. We may militantly fight anyone who challenges it (Nickerson, 1998). This is, unfortunately, how most people operate and why it can be hard to get along in groups and organizations. It's also why openness to experience and curiosity – a beginner's mind – are so important if we're to create healthier work cultures, adapt to the 21st century and solve the global challenges we're facing around work and the future of our planet.

While the role of bias in communication is increasingly recognized, the methods for addressing it remain incoherent and most research comes from studying mental health problems. One of the reasons bias is difficult to address is that there is an emotional element to it and emotions are still poorly included in work conversations. Another reason is that people don't yet feel safe to be wrong – it's perceived as a form of failure.

The antidote: psychological safety

It's hard to do good work in a team or organization where trust doesn't exist. On a very primal level, we need to know that the person in front of us is saying the truth (authenticity) and that they'll do what they say they're going to do (integrity). A lack of trust breeds survivalism, including dysfunctional competition, backstabbing and power contests. People experience low job control, effort-reward imbalance and chronic anxiety – a sense of toxicity.

Having spent thousands of hours in transformational conversations with highly committed and competent professionals in a range of sectors (medicine, science, law, finance, energy), work culture appears to have a huge role in people's career decisions. Helena spent a good year weighing up the pros and cons of whether to leave the security of paid employment before becoming an independent professional. She had worked in some of the most pressured and prestigious organizations in the world and was offered promotions and flexible working so she could live in the countryside while working on exciting global projects. Yet the organization she was working in couldn't offer her something she really cared about: a sense of calm and spaciousness. Work felt hectic and unstable. She also felt it was time for something new and more creative.

Helena was clear about her core values. This clarity played a key role in her decision to take a career leap and create something that works better for her and offers more psychological safety. You might have come across the aphorism: people don't leave jobs, they leave bosses. Based on what I've observed speaking with hundreds of people experiencing similar situations, I would rephrase this to: *people don't leave jobs, they leave toxic work cultures*. It's not even that the organization's culture is particularly unfair or acrimonious. It's just that it might not allow for the sense of ease and wellbeing needed for people to do their best work either alone or in teams. So the environment starts to throttle people's deeper potential and creative genius.

Since the industrial revolution, it seems that we've managed to implement standards and norms that create physical safety at work, but not the standards and norms that create a feeling of psychological safety to enable our full cognitive capacities. Interestingly, research by Google and others called Project Aristotle has revealed thought-provoking findings. The research examined over 180 teams at Google to try to understand what distinguished the high performing ones. They found that the best performing teams didn't deliver because of talent, resources or money. Out of 250 factors they examined, the common denominator for outstanding teams was this: psychological safety. Those that lacked it, didn't do so well (Rozovsky, 2015).

What is psychological safety?

Why do employees sometimes remain silent when they should speak up? Why do we hold back suggestions that could save a project from disaster? Evidence suggests it's because we feel it's not safe to engage. The benefit of saying nothing outweighs the benefit of speaking up. When we fear that our ideas will be rejected or tarnish our reputation, or that our bosses will go so far as to penalize us, we keep our heads down and stay quiet, just like the Volkswagen employees who stayed quiet about fudged emissions numbers leading to the 'diesel dupe' scandal (Herway, 2019).

According to Harvard Business School professor Amy Edmondson, who coined the term 'psychological safety', 'it is a belief that one will not be punished or humiliated for speaking up with ideas, questions, concerns or mistakes'. Edmondson's own research in the context of healthcare showed that the best teams have a culture where workers feel able to speak up about medical errors, learn from them and prevent harm to patients. In less effective teams nurses remained silent about the errors they saw (Edmondson, 2018a).

You've probably come across an environment with a lack of psychological safety. It's an environment where competitiveness dominates (people play a zero-sum game, hog credit, talk over one another, devalue each other to improve their own standing, claim superior knowledge through snide criticism and so on). There's a constant sense of threat and manipulative politicking. Imposter Syndrome thrives here, by the way, because you can never be good enough!

If you're fortunate, you may have experienced the opposite – an environment built on psychological safety. It's one where individuals can take risks and be vulnerable in front of each other. Who is on a team matters less than how the team members interact, structure their work and view their contributions. In fact, the Project Aristotle research identified five top factors for outstanding teams. Here they are in order of importance:

1 **Psychological safety:** Can we take risks in this team without feeling insecure or embarrassed?

2 **Dependability:** Can we count on each other to do high quality work on time?

3 **Structure and clarity:** Are goals, roles and execution plans on our team clear?

4 **Meaning of work:** Are we working on something that is personally important for each of us?

5 **Impact of work:** Do we fundamentally believe that the work we're doing matters? (Rozovsky, 2015)

We spend so much time focusing on ensuring that we're up to the job and have the right technical skills and specialist knowledge for solving problems. But we live in a VUCA world: it's Volatile, Uncertain, Complex and Ambiguous. So what teams and individuals need to thrive in 21st-century complexity might go beyond traditional technical skills and a positive attitude.

What we might really need is to nurture work cultures that create safe and supportive spaces to work. That way, our brain's survival mechanism can switch off and more of our higher cognitive capacities can come online. More of our attention and energy can be channelled into innovation and collaboration rather than survival. We can work from our inner genius rather than our inner boss. This gives organizations a far better chance of solving complex 21st-century problems.

The evidence certainly suggests that it's time to outgrow command-and-control industrial work cultures and embrace more humane principles of relating that make people feel valued and optimize human talent (Barton *et al*, 2012) – a radical but promising transformation of our relational matrix at work. While it's challenging to put hard numbers for the return on the investment of fostering psychological safety, it would be hard to argue against it. It's hard to imagine any organization that couldn't benefit from 'more candour, less denial, richer communication, conscious development of talent, and disciplined leaders, who show compassion for people' (Sherman and Freas, 2004).

Creating work cultures built on psychological safety

With new research like Project Aristotle, there's a glimmer of hope. We can understand what we're trying to work towards. The past 200 to 300 years improved physical safety for employees dramatically. Now we can focus on psychological safety with a view to truly unleashing human genius. With the rapid changes resulting from technological innovation, it's hard to make predictions. But we can at least shift our own attitudes and align with a future where a sense of fulfilment in work is a norm rather than a privilege.

This isn't a distant utopia. As an example, a mid-size US manufacturing company was able to create psychological safety for its employees during a very challenging time and reaped the benefits within two years. The 2008 recession had hit the company hard. It lost 30 per cent of its business and needed to save US $10 million. But the CEO didn't see this as a reason to condone mass layoffs of employees. For him it wasn't logical to think of staff in terms of headcount that dehumanized employees. He reframed it as a 'heartcount' and made a point that everybody mattered (Delach Leonard, 2014)

So he started a Furlough programme where everyone in the company had to take four weeks of unpaid leave whenever they wanted and however they wanted. The way he announced it was that 'it was better that everyone suffer a little than any one person suffer a lot'. Over the year, morale improved and the company made US $20 million in savings (double its target). But the most interesting thing was that rather than getting into a survival mentality, people started to cooperate with each other. Those who could afford to take longer periods of unpaid leave swapped with those who couldn't.

This story and many others challenge the myth that economic imperatives trump humanism, or that the two are mutually exclusive. Compassionate and visionary leaders can help to challenge old myths around performance and efficiency. Failing to do so can spell disaster for individual companies as well as stunting the evolution of 21st-century work culture.

In her book *The Fearless Organization: Creating psychological safety in the workplace for learning, innovation, and growth*, Edmondson reviews a number of case studies and the wider research showing how failure to speak up or push back in an organization contributes to embarrassing failures, such as those at Volkswagen, The Federal Reserve Bank of New York and Nokia. She also cites case studies demonstrating how organizations that have worked hard to create psychological safety – such as clothing line Eileen Fisher, filmmaker Pixar and global manufacturing supplier Barry-Wehmiller – thrive because employees feel they can speak up, offer ideas and ask questions without fear of punishment or embarrassment (Edmondson, 2018b).

We're starting to see the emergence of a positive organizational psychology. But it's only the beginning. If organizations continue to bury their heads in the sand, population growth, rapid economic development and failure to distribute the benefits of technology may result in further dissatisfaction and unrest among the workforce. Dysfunctional competition may continue to provide a breeding ground for anxiety, depression, imposter syndrome, rescuism and burnout. We live in an era where highly experienced doctors working at board level still complain of experiencing a culture of 'fear and intimidation' at board level for years, and where healthcare staff don't feel valued, respected or supported in carrying out very stressful work. Reforming toxic work cultures remains urgent and invaluable (Sturrock, 2018).

Spot good leaders to work with

There's no doubt that there are many leaders in positions of great power who display pathological behaviours (De Haan, 2014). Supporting a culture of psychological safety doesn't mean being naïve. It's important to remain aware and respond to pathological behaviours appropriately.

But what makes a good boss? The best bosses help you feel safe so you can experiment and take risks. They give you the sense of a safe base to leap from and return to with results you're confident to share. When we were children we did best at exploring the world and balancing experimentation and safety when we had a trustworthy base (parent) to come back to between explorations (Bowlby, 1988). Similarly, we need to trust that the person leading us is not going to throw us under a bus to save themselves and abandon us in the lurch. That way we can really put ourselves on the line and do our best and most passionate work. This is born out empirically in extreme situations, for example, in the military.

The Navy SEALs, who run one of the toughest military programmes in the world, train their teams to work together so that any member knows their life is in safe hands. They can risk their lives for others because they know others will do the same for them. As Simon Sinek says in his talk on why great leaders make you feel safe, 'Great leaders would never sacrifice the people to save the numbers; they would sooner sacrifice the numbers to save the people' and in relation to fostering creativity and innovation, 'The role of a leader is not to come up with all the great ideas. The role of a leader is to create an environment in which great ideas can happen' (Sinek, 2014).

So this sense that a person 'has your back' is probably the most important trait to scan for in a leader. Additional traits I've seen in good leaders include the following:

1 **Embracing uncertainty and staying open:** We live in a VUCA world – a constant sense of uncertainty that requires us to become comfortable with the discomfort of uncertainty. By acclimatizing to VUCA, we can retain an open mind and come up with solutions.
2 **Self-leading before leading others:** Awareness (and self-awareness) is key to mastering our motivations and actions. Bad leaders blame others and try to control them. Good leaders know

themselves and therefore have better relationships. They start with self-leadership before leading others. They eventually move to leaderless-leadership where it's not about them or what they do – they flow with what's needed in the moment, stepping in or out as needed.

3 **Going first and eating last:** In a situation of fear and uncertainty, good leaders will take a risk and go first but they will never claim that as a reason for privilege or status. It's their job.

4 **Guiding rather than commanding:** In a VUCA world, command-and-control is ineffective. People's genius needs to be unleashed through wise guidance (and psychological safety).

5 **Knowing when to let go:** In a VUCA world, it's hard to predict outcomes. Sometimes a project or programme strategy is broken. Knowing when to let go and stop asking employees to rearrange the deckchairs on the *Titanic* is wisdom in action.

6 **Compassionate ruthlessness:** Balancing credibility and connection is at the heart of the art of influence. Good leaders support everyone they work with but see the big picture with ruthless clarity. They do the inner work necessary to release limiting assumptions and biases, and they master their energy.

LEADING BY BEING VULNERABLE FIRST

Something that creates human connection rapidly is sharing something that you don't want people to know about you. We're used to sharing things that we're proud of or know are acceptable (things we want people to know about us): our credentials, achievements, etc. Balancing this with sharing more vulnerable information will change the dynamic in a group very quickly and help people open up. As an exercise in a team meeting, try the following:

- Go around the table and ask everyone to share one thing they would like others to know (eg a strength that they know the team can rely on or a recent success): 'Say your name and one thing you'd like people to know about you'.

- Go around again and ask them this time to share one thing they don't want others to know. 'Say your name and one thing you don't want people to know about you'.

  Always go first as the team leader. It's also important that you share something authentically that came to you during the meeting (not something you prepared earlier). Acknowledge everyone for their honesty and courage. Ask them how it felt to start the meeting that way and notice any change in the energy in the room.

Healthy human productivity

The word productivity is used to indicate efficiency. *Productivity is a measure of output compared with input. Being productive* suggests that you're able to 'do more with less'. While this sounds sensible, much of the turmoil in work culture can be attributed to a sense of being squeezed to achieve more with fewer resources and less time. But humans cannot be reduced to a machine-like state of productivity – simply converting energy into outputs based on an algorithm. That's a perfect job for a machine but not for a human. In some ways, it's the inevitable culmination of the industrial revolution that began over 200 years ago. But we don't have to follow that trajectory. It's great if we can create technology that maximizes the conversion of energy into output. But as humans, we need a sense of freedom to create and do our best work. Here are a few principles and distinctions to help you cultivate a sense of freedom, even if you work in a culture that treats humans like machines.

Spaciousness and the courage of a not-to-do list

The use of the word productivity in reference to a person ('quality of being productive') appears to date back to 1809 (Origin and

190

meaning of productivity, nd). Around the same time, the 'to-do list' was born, with Benjamin Franklin's 1791 to-do list being the first recorded instance. His to-do list opened with the question 'What good shall I do this day?' (Zantal-Wiener, 2017). Is it a coincidence that the to-do list was born during the industrial revolution? Regardless of the causes, the to-do list has become less of an aid for us to create ways of being of service, and more of a shackle.

Productivity psychology points to the advantages of having a *not-to-do* list. This is to make sure you stay away from the many things you might be tempted to do that scatter your focus and energy without helping you create what you want in your day (Zetlin, 2020). Remember Warren Buffett's advice to his pilot? Pick your top five must do's in life and put everything else, including the sort-of-would-be-good-to-do stuff, on another list called 'stay away from at all costs'.

But the to-do list discussion begs the question of why we have one in the first place. Why are we motivated to put things on a list and have that dictate how we spend our time? Clearly, there's a healthy element to putting your thoughts on paper. But the modern tendency to fill up our time has been linked to fear – fear of freedom. We get anxious if we feel empty or bored even if there's no reason to be and you could simply enjoy sitting quietly and breathing for a while. We're afraid of missing out or falling behind. So it requires courage to settle into that emptiness or boredom and use it as an opportunity to rest or self-reflect. Allowing yourself some space may be the scariest thing you ever do if you're a busy high achiever, but it will provide you with rich rewards, as we've discussed in Part Two.

DO ONE THING THAT SCARES YOU EVERY DAY
Drop one thing, even if it scares you, every day

Taking a small step in the direction of fear rather than resisting it by distracting yourself is called *leaning into your edge*. Leaning into

---

your edge may bring you face-to-face with a limiting belief about what you can or can't do in work, relationships and life.

1 What are you afraid of? Challenge the assumptions you hold about it (use the HAPI process); step into the fear one small step at a time.

2 Equally, what are you doing that you want to stop? Perhaps it drains you, upsets you or is just an unhelpful habit? It might feel scary, but you know fear is simply an unquestioned thought.

3 What will you create today? An experience of freedom, peace or authenticity? Perhaps you'll share a message in writing or by speaking up?

You can't get it wrong! You're just living in alignment with what's true for you. Remember to celebrate your efforts and courage!

The vocational life versus work–life balance

The term 'work–life balance' originated relatively recently. It was first used in the UK and the United States in the late 1970s and 1980s. It generally describes satisfaction and good functioning at work and at home, with a minimum of role conflict (Rantanen *et al*, 2011). Where I grew up, concepts like 'socializing' and 'hobbies' didn't exist. Connecting with people and taking time to savour the moment were woven into the workday. These are differences between individualistic societies and more community-oriented ones, as well as between agricultural societies where people live on the land and have no set working hours, and industrial ones with a clear demarcation between places of work and personal life.

Over a lifetime you might notice that there is no such thing as work–life balance. Sometimes work takes precedence and sometimes your personal life does. It's more of an ongoing conversation informed by your creative cycles and the organic rhythms of life. The problem is when the conversation stops and work becomes a compulsion encouraged by the work culture. Poet David Whyte describes this poignantly in his books *The Three Marriages: Reimagining work, self and relationship* (2009) and *The Heart Aroused: Poetry and the preservation of the soul in corporate America* (1994). If you feel chained to work or that you're struggling to keep all your plates spinning, it's time to explore what's going on. Perhaps you're trying to meet too many external expectations of success.

A vocation is an occupation to which a person is especially drawn or for which they are suited, trained or qualified. It derives from the Old French *vocacion* 'call, consecration; calling, profession' or directly from Latin *vocatio*, literally 'a calling, a being called'. Living vocationally does not imply that you have to join a monastery. But you might discover your true vocation if you're willing to step outside the Success Trap, once you've let go of the weight of external expectations. You might find that you're drawn to a completely different career or a new way of engaging with the work you're already doing.

What you're drawn to becomes your organizing principle in life. If you're drawn to material success, your life will be organized around that. If you're drawn to fame and power, your life will be organized around that. If you're drawn to creativity and peace, things will look different again. What you're drawn to becomes your organizing principle in life and it's internally fuelled not externally imposed. Usually people slow down dramatically once they break out of the Success Trap (although some speed up if they were stuck and procrastinating). Once they're off the treadmill, they can recover a more organic pace of life. Your vocation might simply be to take your time doing what needs to be done, no more and no less.

Acclimatize to spaciousness

One of our modern diseases is a lack of inner space, from being saturated with information, thoughts, emotions and all manner of mental stimulation. You may have heard the word 'spacious-ness', or perhaps you know what that feels like, intuitively. One way to think about spaciousness is that it's the opposite of clut-ter. When you enter a room with too many things in it, or an office with papers and books all over the place, you know what a cluttered space feels like.

You may have had the sensation of being 'too close' to a situ-ation or person, needing to get away from it and put some distance between you. There isn't enough 'psychological distance' between you and the next object. Sometimes, people go on retreat to rediscover this sense of spaciousness. It can be quite tough to slow down from the hectic pace of life (the mind has a hard time letting go of constant stimulation and activity), but within a few days, they reconnect to a sense of peace and calm and wonder why they would ever live any other way...

In addition to feeling rather pleasant, spaciousness appears to give us more resilience in the face of distress. In experiments at Yale University on the impact of spaciousness, participants were asked to draw two points on a piece of paper. The participants who drew them far apart (a prompt for spaciousness) were more resilient to a distressing image or stimulus than those who drew the two points closer. It's thought that spaciousness gives us more capacity to feel safe and therefore calm in any situation, because we feel psycho-logically at a distance from the threat (Herbert, 2008).

Spaciousness isn't just a nice-to-have. Aside from enhancing resilience it has also been found to foster creativity including through exposure to vast natural landscapes either directly or through images (Van Rompay and Jol, 2016). Creativity is deemed to be the most prized skill by leaders in the 21st century (IBM, 2010). Yet organizations often fail to provide the right environment to foster this higher cognitive functioning while asking people to innovate. Work culture expectations are still clustered around analysis and busy task delivery rather than the spaciousness and calm needed for that kind of spontaneous brilliance.

Whether it's writing something, a difficult conversation or playing with your kids, spaciousness changes the quality of your attention and energy. It's another reason for slowing down, lightening your schedule and prioritizing what truly matters. By doing this for ourselves we take a stand for work culture to transform.

Don't compete, play an infinite game

Success becomes a trap if we chase it. It ensnares us if we treat it as though it's somewhere to get to and that once achieved, brings us victory. This illusion is what drives us to struggle and elbow people out of the way. Philosopher James Carse calls this version of success a finite game and distinguishes it from the much bigger infinite game that we can play in work and life (Carse, 2012; Sinek, 2019). Finite games have a beginning and an end. For example, in many sports the person with most points wins. Both players can't win. Similarly, you might go to an interview knowing that only one person can get the job. Either you get the job or someone else does. But what if careers, business and leadership weren't finite but infinite games?

Infinite games do not have an end. The game continues even after the players have finished. Life continues even after we die. Similarly, work, business, technology will all continue after we're gone. So we can relax and enjoy being part of the game for a while. We can add a few notes to the great symphony.

So next time you feel nervous about a talk, interview or appraisal, while it may feel like a life-and-death situation, remember it's just a few extra notes in the symphony – a small movement of a much bigger, much vaster universal game that you get to play. In an infinite game, you can't lose because the only rule is to do your best and keep playing until you're gone. Sometimes you may be ahead and at other times you might feel behind. But the game continues.

If you knew you were part of something bigger and that your career or business wasn't a matter of life and death but an opportunity to offer your best and be part of something much bigger than you, what becomes possible? Perhaps the impossible starts to become possible. Many a career shifter has achieved something much greater by letting go of conventional success. Both Gandhi and Nelson Mandela abandoned their legal careers, for example. Perhaps you can make space for an *impossible goal* like ending poverty or compassionate politics. The end goal isn't the point. It's about the fulfilment that comes from giving our energies to something greater than ourselves.

You don't have to do it alone

High achievers tend to be so competent they forget what it's like to work with others or even how to ask for help. Depending on other people's support (rather than rescuing them) can feel alien or even debilitatingly vulnerable. They prefer independence, sometimes to their own detriment. Working with the wrong people can drain your energy and make you feel isolated. The right people can help you feel buoyed and supported as you allow your wings to spread. The right people will see your deeper potential even when you can't. They'll reflect back the possibilities and celebrate the steps you take. They'll be right there with you on the worst days reminding you of your hopes, dreams and gifts.

You don't have to be surrounded by a large number of people. Those who inspire you don't even have to be people you know personally. In *The 10 Laws of Career Reinvention: Essential survival skills for any economy*, Pamela Mitchell suggests having a Career Reinvention Board – peers, colleagues, friends, mentors (Mitchell, 2011). The number of people doesn't matter. It's the impact they have on you that counts. One person might be there for support, another because they're good at noticing your blind spots, and yet another because they know about the type of work you want to do. Building a community of people who can both show you what's possible and challenge you to go beyond your limiting beliefs with compassionate ruthlessness is invaluable. Slowing down in your interactions so you can connect with people at a deeper level (beneath the surface patterns of behaviour and speech) and see what's needed in an interaction makes your relationships a wonderful space for creativity, care and freedom.

Living from a sense of freedom together

Hopefully by now you are willing if not looking forward to embracing uncertainty and tuning into the sense of possibility and freedom uncertainty carries with it. Work doesn't have to be drudgery or struggle. Fulfilment and freedom are closer than you think. They're one limiting belief or fearful emotion away and both of these can be addressed with enquiry into your thoughts and mastery of your emotions. Your limiting thoughts and beliefs may have served you in the past – creating a Success Trap precisely because they were useful – but it's time to let them go so you can unleash your genius and fulfil your potential at a deeper level. You may have to step outside a toxic environment to really focus on you and what you really want. But the most important thing is the initial spark of possibility that tells you something else is possible.

Of course, these words can seem all but true when you're right in the middle of uncertainty and struggle. So you may just have to trust me for a moment when I say: you can make it! Breaking out of the Success Trap requires courage and attention. Once you're on the other side, a new journey begins. Maintaining your freedom of mind becomes a way of life. It's like Russian dolls. Every time you open one you feel a little freer and happier, and a little more connected to your deeper values. But you may find one doll reveals another. Each doll is a limiting belief you can break open to see more clearly.

With time you become better at reading the terrain outside the success trap and the challenges you meet simply become a reflection of limiting beliefs you might hold. It's what poet Paul Eluard called 'the solemn geographies of human limits' (Eluard, 2005). You've become your own teacher, mentor and guide outside the Success Trap, as well as being able to ask for and receive help from trusted others. You're more discerning of which bosses and organizations are healthy. Most importantly, you're the source of your own happiness and that is the ultimate success.

Conclusion

'It always appears impossible until it's done'

So here you are. You've made it to the end of the book – but the journey goes on. Perhaps it's only the beginning of a career transformation for you. Perhaps you're in the messy middle. Perhaps when you began this book, you were concerned about your career direction or felt that you were wasting time and not fulfilling your potential. Now, you may have reconnected with your bigger vision and something much vaster to inspire you. If not, don't worry. Everything comes in its own right time. Keep doing the work to question your assumptions and stay curious about what's possible.

About a billion people are unfulfilled at work. According to Gallup's Global State of the Workplace survey that we discussed in Chapter 1, 85 per cent of employees are 'not engaged' or are 'actively disengaged' at work, indicating that the majority of the global workforce are unhappy. They estimate a loss of US $7trillion in productivity, not to mention the lost human potential.

The cause of this global unhappiness? According to the report:

> [t]he new workforce is looking for things like purpose, opportunities to develop, ongoing conversations, a coach rather than a boss, and a manager who leverages their strengths rather than obsessing over their weaknesses. They see work and life as interconnected, and they want their job to be a part of their identity.

Reforming global corporate culture is a long-term solution. Good leaders and healthy organizational cultures can help, but we can't rely on external circumstances for happiness. That's just another trap. So what can you do in the meantime? Spending too much time cogitating over the ideal job, business strategy or finding your purpose and values is not the optimal use of your time. In fact, letting go of the need to find your purpose is immensely liberating. You can build on your career capital and successfully launch into a new career or build a business while figuring it out as you go along. All the while, you can allow for more time for rest, relationships, creativity and anything else you deeply value and makes life worthwhile.

One thing is certain: life is always changing. But a sense of flow and fulfilment in work requires awareness and the courage to exercise choice. We need to do the inner work to break free of limiting beliefs, identities and cultural myths, and unlearn what is no longer adapted to 21st-century uncertainty. Incorporating this understanding into daily working life frees up our energy and our genius. It also frees us from the limiting misconceptions of the Success Trap. Then we can go through the creative cycles of our work and lives with more joy.

In many ways, the Success Trap is our larger human story. We're at the top of the food chain, but our way of living, with its never-ending quest for more, threatens to destroy our environment and ourselves in the process. By questioning our socially constructed identities we can embrace new possibilities and break free of the Success Trap. As a result, we start contributing to the radical reinvention of the social and cultural fabric of our civilization away from greed and fear and towards more compassion, generosity and wisdom.

No amount of material security or external validation is going to give you the certainty your mammalian-reptilian brain instincts seek. The courage to look within and differentiate between the real limitations in life (its inherent uncertainty, loss, and eventually death) and your perceived limitations will help you break free of any trap you've inadvertently constructed for yourself. The certainty you seek can simply come from the knowledge that you can face whatever life throws at you and commit to doing your best with the capacities you have.

Give yourself space and time to listen and hear your inner genius. Let it help you articulate and resolve the inner conflicts of 21st-century work and life. With space, you can resolve the paradox of how your old success gets in the way of your new success. When you're feeling stuck or trapped give yourself a moment to pause and ask yourself: *What assumptions am I making in this moment? How are they unhelpful?* It takes patience and compassion to challenge the limiting assumptions, identities and cultural myths we've picked up over a lifetime. With compassionate ruthlessness, your willingness to resolve any confusion will carry you through and out of the trap.

One thing I've noticed is that life takes an upswing when I find myself doing something and thinking this: *I would rather do this from a cardboard box than not do it.* That's how I know my purpose, or at least the next step in my purpose, has revealed itself. Don't ask what job might make you feel good and pay you well. Ask what you're willing to fail for and do more of that. You can take heart in knowing that failure and success are part of the same journey. If you're failing, you are much closer to success than you think. The more you're willing to fail and be open to learning from the experience, the more you can succeed on your own terms and be free. With that you'll have shifted from an employee to an entrepreneurial mindset, which is arguably the future of work for humans, especially as machines take over repetitive, non-creative tasks and leave us with the complex ones that the intangible human genius is best suited to.

Giving yourself permission to move forward with the principles that have resonated for you in this book will help guide you onto a new trajectory even if it's not fully formed in your mind yet. You don't have to wait for a dream job or make a lot of money to break out of the trap. Let your purpose reveal itself as you live with authenticity and integrity. You are made of that kind of courage. In the hardest times when I've wanted to give up and the world seemed like a dark place, I've taken heart from Nelson Mandela's words: *It always seems impossible until it's done.*

Bibliography

Chapter One

80000 (2019) [accessed 2 February 2020] About us: 80,000 Hours [Online] https://80000hours.org/about/ (archived at https://perma.cc/6ZWA-U3BN)

Anderson, B (2020) [accessed 5 February 2020] The most in-demand hard and soft skills of 2020, LinkedIn Talent Blog [Online] https://business.linkedin.com/talent-solutions/blog/trends-and-research/2020/most-in-demand-hard-and-soft-skills (archived at https://perma.cc/96EN-FUDS)

Barrett, H (2017) [accessed 2 February 2020] Plan for five careers in a lifetime, *Financial Times* [Online] www.ft.com/content/0151d2fe-868a-11e7-8bb1-5ba57d47eff7 (archived at https://perma.cc/P5T5-AWSK)

Bennett, N and Lemoine, GJ (2014) [accessed 11 January 2020] What VUCA really means for you, *Harvard Business Review* [Online] https://hbr.org/2014/01/what-vuca-really-means-for-you (archived at https://perma.cc/ZTP9-L3UT)

Brynjolfsson, E and McAfee, A (2014) *The Second Machine Age: Work, progress, and prosperity in a time of brilliant technologies*, W. W. Norton & Company, New York

Bryson, A and MacKerron, G (2017) Are you happy while you work? *The Economic Journal*, **127** (599), pp 106–25

Clifford, C (2016) [accessed 2 February 2020] Elon Musk: Robots will take your jobs, government will have to pay your wage, *CNBC* [Online] www.cnbc.com/2016/11/04/elon-musk-robots-will-take-your-jobs-government-will-have-to-pay-your-wage.html (archived at https://perma.cc/Q6RA-653Y)

Cook, J (2018) [accessed 2 February 2020] One in three GPs likely to quit within five years, warns RCGP [Online] www.gponline.com/one-three-gps-likely-quit-within-five-years-warns-rcgp/article/1520103 (archived at https://perma.cc/JN38-T43D)

De Neve, J-E and Ward, G (2017) [accessed 13 April 2020] Happiness at work [Online] http://cep.lse.ac.uk/pubs/download/dp1474.pdf (archived at https://perma.cc/FH6B-AWWS)

Gallup (2017) [accessed 13 April 2020] State of the Global Workplace [Online] www.slideshare.net/adrianboucek/state-of-the-global-workplace-gallup-report-2017 (archived at https://perma.cc/6M68-LPBC)

Helliwell, JF, Layard, R and Sachs, JD (2019) [accessed 8 April 2020] World Happiness Report 2019, Sustainable Solutions Network [Online] https://worldhappiness.report/ed/2019/#read (archived at https://perma.cc/V932-ECH7)

Hitchcock, A, Laycock, K and Sundorph, E (2017) [accessed 2 January 2020] Work in progress: Towards a leaner, smarter public-sector workforce [Online] https://reform.uk/research/work-progress-towards-leaner-smarter-public-sector-workforce (archived at https://perma.cc/F83K-HTM3)

McKinsey & Co (2017) [accessed 23 September 2020] Jobs lost, jobs gained: What the future of work will mean for jobs, skills, and wages [Online] https://www.mckinsey.com/featured-insights/future-of-work/jobs-lost-jobs-gained-what-the-future-of-work-will-mean-for-jobs-skills-and-wages (archived at https://perma.cc/M3T2-VHQC)

UN (2019) [accessed 2 February 2020] Special edition: Progress towards the Sustainable Development Goals Report of the Secretary-General [Online] https://undocs.org/E/2019/68 (archived at https://perma.cc/F8ZL-HABL)

Usborne, S (2014) [accessed 2 February 2020] Why a career is no longer for life, The Independent [Online] www.independent.co.uk/voices/comment/why-a-career-is-no-longer-for-life-9032851.html (archived at https://perma.cc/DD9T-BJF7)

WEF (2017) [accessed 2 February 2020] The Inclusive Growth and Development Report 2017 Insight Report [Online] www3.weforum.org/docs/WEF_Forum_IncGrwth_2017.pdf (archived at https://perma.cc/4NFT-2HVB)

Chapter Two

Barr, S (2018) [accessed 2 February 2020] This is how much money you need to earn to be happy, according to new study, The Independent [Online] www.independent.co.uk/life-style/money-happiness-how-much-earnings-income-needed-study-perdue-university-indiana-gallup-world-poll-a8218086.html (archived at https://perma.cc/PRV8-4NZR)

Blanchflower, DG and Oswald, AJ (2008) Is well-being U-shaped over the life cycle? *Social Science and Medicine*, **66** (8), pp 1733–49

Dwyer, KK and Davidson, MM (2012) Is public speaking really more feared than death? *Communication Research Reports*, **29** (2), pp 99–107

Edmonson, A (2018) [accessed 15 January 2020] The importance of psychological safety, *HR Magazine* [Online] www.hrmagazine.co.uk/article-details/the-importance-of-psychological-safety (archived at https://perma.cc/2SSQ-U8VK)

Fleming, S (2019) [accessed 4 February 2020] These 4 trends are shaping the future of your job, World Economic Forum [Online] www.weforum.org/agenda/2019/02/these-4-trends-are-shaping-the-future-of-your-job/ (archived at https://perma.cc/RH5U-QDW7)

Gallo, C (2018) [accessed 2 February 2020] Research shows this is the ideal age to start a business, *Business Insider* [Online] www.businessinsider.com/research-shows-this-is-the-ideal-age-to-start-a-business-2018-2?r=US&IR=T (archived at https://perma.cc/9LDJ-BBHD)

IBM (2010) [accessed 4 January 2020] Capitalizing on Complexity: Insights from the Global Chief Executive Officer Study [Online] www.ibm.com/downloads/cas/1VZV5X8J (archived at https://perma.cc/N2GQ-PZJT)

Jebb, AT *et al* (2018) Happiness, income satiation and turning points around the world, *Nature Human Behaviour*, **2** (1), pp 33–38

Joubert, JHM and Rothmann, S (2007) Job demands, job resources, burnout and work engagement of managers at a platinum mine in the North West Province, *South African Journal of Business Management – Sabinet*, **38** (3), pp 49–61

Korczak, D and Huber, B (2012) Burn-out: Kann Man es Messen? *Bundesgesundheitsblatt – Gesundheitsforschung – Gesundheitsschutz*, **55** (2), pp 164–71

Layard, R (2011) *Happiness: Lessons from a new science*, Penguin, London

Marmot, M (2015) *Status Syndrome: How your place on the social gradient directly affects your health*, 1st edn, Bloomsbury Paperbacks, London

Mayo Clinic (2018) [accessed 2 February 2020] Job burnout: How to spot it and take action [Online] www.mayoclinic.org/healthy-lifestyle/adult-health/in-depth/burnout/art-20046642 (archived at https://perma.cc/YPG7-RKKQ)

Norman, SB and Maguen, S (2020) [accessed 2 February 2020] Moral injury. PTSD: National Center for PTSD [Online] https://www.ptsd. va.gov/professional/treat/cooccurring/moral_injury.asp (archived at https://perma.cc/GBT9-9UJ9)

Raedeke, TD, Granzyk, TL and Warren, A (2000) Why coaches experience burnout: A commitment perspective, *Journal of Sport and Exercise Psychology*, **22** (1), pp 85–105

Robinson, OC and Wright, GRT (2013) The prevalence, types and perceived outcomes of crisis episodes in early adulthood and midlife, *International Journal of Behavioral Development*, **37** (5), pp 407–16

Rose, A (2019) [accessed 13 April 2020] The Alison Rose Review of Female Entrepreneurship [Online] https://assets.publishing.service.gov.uk/ government/uploads/system/uploads/attachment_data/file/784324/ RoseReview_Digital_FINAL.PDF (archived at https://perma.cc/N2ZF-S94T)

Schwab, K (2016) [accessed 2 February 2020] The Fourth Industrial Revolution: What it means and how to respond, World Economic Forum [Online] www.weforum.org/agenda/2016/01/the-fourth-industrial-revolution-what-it-means-and-how-to-respond/ (archived at https://perma.cc/8FQ8-Z8VE)

Schwandt, H (2015) [accessed 2 February 2020] Why so many of us experience a midlife crisis, *Harvard Business Review* [Online] https:// hbr.org/2015/04/why-so-many-of-us-experience-a-midlife-crisis (archived at https://perma.cc/RHY2-SVK6)

Schwartz, T (2010) [accessed 2 February 2020] The Productivity Myth, *Harvard Business Review* [Online] https://hbr.org/2010/05/the-productivity-myth-2 (archived at https://perma.cc/TK8J-2DLC)

Simovic, D (2019) [accessed 5 February 2020] 39 Entrepreneur statistics you need to know in 2020, Smallbizgenius [Online] www. smallbizgenius.net/by-the-numbers/entrepreneur-statistics/#gref (archived at https://perma.cc/7XTY-RZCB)

Sinek, S (2017) *Leaders Eat Last: Why some teams pull together and others don't*, Penguin, London

Stout, L (2012) *The Shareholder Value Myth*, Penguin Random House, London

Usborne, S (2014) [accessed 2 February 2020] Why a career is no longer for life, *The Independent* [Online] www.independent.co.uk/voices/ comment/why-a-career-is-no-longer-for-life-9032851.html (archived at https://perma.cc/BF5X-VMHY)

Weber, M and Swedberg, R (2009) *The Protestant Ethic and the Spirit of Capitalism: The Talcott Parsons translation interpretations*, W.W. Norton & Co, New York

Chapter Three

AHRQ (2019) [accessed 2 February 2020] Fatigue, sleep deprivation, and patient safety, *PSNet* [Online] https://psnet.ahrq.gov/primer/fatigue-sleep-deprivation-and-patient-safety (archived at https://perma.cc/5W89-74Z4)

Bronson, P (2007) [accessed 2 February 2020] How not to talk to your kids, *New York Magazine* [Online] http://nymag.com/news/features/27840/ (archived at https://perma.cc/8B4Q-PCEU)

Coffey, H (2017) [accessed 2 February 2020] Hypoxia definition - why adults SHOULD do their oxygen mask BEFORE a child's on a flight, *The Express* [Online] www.express.co.uk/travel/articles/758140/hypoxia-definition-flight-mask (archived at https://perma.cc/YQP3-7UUS)

Dweck, C (1999) [accessed 2 February 2020] Caution: Praise can be dangerous, *American Educator – American Federation of Teachers* [Online] www.aft.org/sites/default/files/periodicals/PraiseSpring99.pdf (archived at https://perma.cc/B8QD-63RX)

Edmonson, AC (2018) *The Fearless Organization: Creating psychological safety in the workplace for learning, innovation, and growth*, John Wiley & Sons, New York

Frankl, VE (1988) *The Will to Meaning: Foundations and applications of logotherapy*, Penguin, London

Franklin, RC and Pearn, JH (2011) Drowning for love: The aquatic victim-instead-of-rescuer syndrome – Drowning fatalities involving those attempting to rescue a child, *Journal of Paediatrics and Child Health*, 47 (1–2), pp 44–47

Fromm, E (2001) *The Fear of Freedom*, Routledge, Oxford

García, H (2017) *Ikigai: The Japanese secret to a long and happy life*, Hutchinson, London

Hoang, Q (2013) [accessed 2 February 2020] The Impostor Phenomenon: Overcoming internalized barriers and recognizing achievements, *The Vermont Connection*, 34 (1), Article 6 [Online] https://scholarworks.uvm.edu/tvc/vol34/iss1/6 (archived at https://perma.cc/SN3Y-3DBT)

Kets de Vries, MFR (2012) Leadership coaching and the Rescuer Syndrome: How to manage both sides of the couch, *SSRN Electronic Journal*, doi: 10.2139/ssrn.1722610

Rose, P, Suzanne, C and Imes, A (1978) The impostor phenomenon in high achieving women: Dynamics and therapeutic intervention, *Psychotherapy: Theory, Research and Practice*, **15** (3), pp 241–47

Sampson, JP *et al* (2000) Using readiness assessment to improve career services: A cognitive information-processing approach, *The Career Development Quarterly*, **49** (2), pp 146–74

Sandel, M (2020) [accessed 2 February 2020] Justice (Course), Boston, Harvard University [Online] https://online-learning.harvard.edu/course/justice (archived at https://perma.cc/N7NZ-N9CH)

Sprague, S (2017) [accessed 2 February 2020] Below trend: The U.S. productivity slowdown since the Great Recession – Beyond the numbers, *U.S. Bureau of Labor Statistics*, **6** (2) [Online] www.bls.gov/opub/btn/volume-6/below-trend-the-us-productivity-slowdown-since-the-great-recession.htm (archived at https://perma.cc/6WM9-RRZV)

Steiner, S (2012) [accessed 2 February 2020] Top five regrets of the dying, *The Guardian* [Online] www.theguardian.com/lifeandstyle/2012/feb/01/top-five-regrets-of-the-dying (archived at https://perma.cc/R7FS-FCEP)

Taylor, B (2019) [accessed 2 February 2020] The productivity myth: How modern companies are getting work wrong, Dropbox Blog [Online] https://blog.dropbox.com/topics/work-culture/productivity-myth-getting-work-wrong (archived at https://perma.cc/HRQ7-8GKP)

TheHubEvents (2019) [accessed 2 February 2020] Impostor Syndrome Survey Results [Online] www.thehubevents.com/resources/impostor-syndrome-survey-results-116/ (archived at https://perma.cc/98AA-C9L9)

Winston, CN (2015) International contributions points of convergence and divergence between existential and humanistic psychology: A few observations, *The Humanistic Psychologist*, **43** (1), 40–53

Chapter Four

Clarine, S (nd) [accessed 4 February 2020] Crush your goals like a Navy SEAL: 4 guaranteed ways to step up and make progress, *One Idea*

Away [Online] www.oneideaaway.com/develop-micro-goals/ (archived at https://perma.cc/2HJ6-5YC7)

Csikszentmihályi, M (1990) *Flow: The psychology of optimal experience*, Harper & Row, New York

Csikszentmihályi, M (2013) *Flow: The psychology of happiness*, Ebury Digital, London

Fullagar, CJ and Kelloway, EK (2009) Flow at work: An experience sampling approach, *Journal of Occupational and Organizational Psychology*, **82** (3), pp 595–615

Gardner, S and Albee, D (2013) [accessed 8 April 2020] Dominican Research cited in *Forbes* article [Online] https://scholar.dominican.edu/news-releases/386 (archived at https://perma.cc/M4RR-QXVF)

Gilbert, D (2006) Stumbling on Happiness, A. A. Knopf, New York

Ibarra, H (2003) *Working Identity: Unconventional strategies for reinventing your career*, Harvard Business School Press, Harvard, MA

IBM (2010) [accessed 8 April 2020] *Capitalizing on Complexity: Insights from the Global Chief Executive Officer Study* [Online] www.ibm.com/downloads/cas/1VZV5X8J (archived at https://perma.cc/6RZF-HBXP)

Jacobs, D (2017) *Banish Your Inner Critic: Silence the voice of self-doubt to unleash your creativity and do your best work*, Mango Publishing Group, Miami, FL

Kim, K-H (2016) *The Creativity Challenge: How we can recapture American innovation*, Prometheus Books, New York

Limb, CJ and Braun, AR (2008) Neural substrates of spontaneous musical performance: An fMRI study of jazz improvisation, *PLoS ONE*, 3 (2), p. e1679

Maslow, AH (1943) Classics in the history of psychology: A theory of human motivation, originally published in *Psychological Review*, 50, pp 370–96 [Online] http://psychclassics.yorku.ca/Maslow/motivation.htm (archived at https://perma.cc/2LYT-9KKF)

McCartney, P (2019) [accessed 6 February 2020] What is the story behind The Beatles' *Let It Be?* Radio X, *James Corden Show* [Online] www.radiox.co.uk/artists/beatles/let-it-be-meaning-story-lyrics/ (archived at https://perma.cc/HD7D-9DFX)

Meister, J (2012) [accessed 2 January 2020] The future of work: Job hopping is the 'new normal' for Millennials [Online] www.forbes.com/sites/jeannemeister/2012/08/14/the-future-of-work-job-hopping-is-the-new-normal-for-millennials/#4d88e7a613b8 (archived at https://perma.cc/H3B7-9VLF)

Murphy, B (2015) [accessed 4 February 2020] 17 things Navy SEALs learn that can help you succeed in life, Inc.com [Online] www.inc.com/ bill-murphy-jr/heres-the-ultimate-navy-seal-guide-to-exceptional-success-and-achievement.html (archived at https://perma.cc/2GKS-RNVF)

Navy SEALs (nd) [accessed 4 February 2020] Hell Week, Navy SEALs [Online] https://navyseals.com/nsw/hell-week-0/ (archived at https:// perma.cc/Q7CA-MV5G)

Oshin, M (nd) [accessed 8 April 2020] Warren Buffett's '3-step' 5/25 strategy: How to focus and prioritize your time like a billionaire, *Mayo Oshin Newsletter* [Online] https://mayooshin.com/buffett-5-25-rule/ (archived at https://perma.cc/GZ6Y-Z5QH)

Ritter, SM and Dijksterhuis, A (2014) Creativity: The unconscious foundations of the incubation period, *Frontiers in Human Neuroscience*, doi: 10.3389/fnhum.2014.00215

Robbins, T (2014) [accessed 4 February 2020] 6 human needs: Do you need to feel significant? *Entrepreneur* [Online] www.tonyrobbins.com/mind-meaning/ do-you-need-to-feel-significant/ (archived at https://perma.cc/3YDJ-DELM)

Scientific American (1997) [accessed 13 April 2020] What is the function of the various brainwaves? [Online] www.scientificamerican.com/ article/what-is-the-function-of-t-1997-12-22/ (archived at https:// perma.cc/2BTQ-YMR9)

Sevilla, GC (2020) [accessed 1 February 2020] 10 skills needed most in 2020 and 30 free courses to learn them, *Entrepreneur* [Online] www. entrepreneur.com/article/344870?utm_source=newsletter&utm_ medium=email (archived at https://perma.cc/D28X-RBKD)

Shimamura, AP (2002) Muybridge in motion: Travels in art, psychology and neurology, *History of Photography*, 26 (4), pp 341–50

Tamir, DI and Mitchell, JP (2012) Disclosing information about the self is intrinsically rewarding, *Proceedings of the National Academy of Sciences of the United States of America*, **109** (21), pp 8038–43

Wallas, G (1926) *The Art of Thought*, Harcourt Brace, New York

Chapter Five

Aronsson, G *et al* (2017) A systematic review including meta-analysis of work environment and burnout symptoms, *BMC Public Health*, **17** (1), doi: 10.1186/s12889-017-4153-7

Bolden-Barrett, V (2019) [accessed 4 February 2020] Worker stress costs employers billions in lost productivity, *HR Dive* [Online] www.hrdive.com/news/worker-stress-costs-employers-billions-in-lost-productivity/550651/ (archived at https://perma.cc/42D4-JG4B)

Buser, T and Peter, N (2011) [accessed 4 February 2020] Multitasking: Productivity effects and gender differences, Tinbergen Institute Discussion Paper 044/3 [Online] www.tinbergen.nl (archived at https://perma.cc/R2FP-JKJU)

Chang, C and Groeneveld, R (2018) [accessed 2 January 2020] Slowing down to speed up, McKinsey & Company blog [Online] www.mckinsey.com/business-functions/organization/our-insights/the-organization-blog/slowing-down-to-speed-up (archived at https://perma.cc/W2M2-KGPQ)

Covey, SR (2012) *The 7 Habits of Highly Effective People*, Simon & Schuster, New York

Dufu, T and Steinem, G (2018) *Drop the Ball: Expect less from yourself and flourish at work & life*, Penguin, London

FourDayWeek (2020) [accessed 4 February 2020] Four-day week trial [Online] https://4dayweek.com/four-day-week-trial (archived at https://perma.cc/P7CL-MM99)

Frietsch, T (2016) [accessed 24 December 2019] Effect of 8 weeks of MBSR training on neuroplasticity and improvement of attention, memory and well-being [Online] https://clinicaltrials.gov/ct2/show/NCT02672761 (archived at https://perma.cc/6P4Z-L6AW)

Goleman, D (1996) *Emotional Intelligence: Why it can matter more than IQ*, Bloomsbury Publishing, New York

Harris, DB (2014) *10% Happier: How I tamed the voice in my head, reduced stress without losing my edge, and found self-help that actually works*, HarperCollins, New York

Harris, D and Happify (nd) [accessed 8 April 2020] The skeptic's guide to meditation [Online] www.happify.com/hd/skeptics-guide-to-meditation-infographic-dan-harris/ (archived at https://perma.cc/D8KH-CR4P)

IBM (2010) [accessed 4 January 2020] Capitalizing on Complexity: Insights from the Global Chief Executive Officer Study [Online] www.ibm.com/downloads/cas/1VZV5X8J (archived at https://perma.cc/T3BD-DMJ3)

Ireland, T (2014) [accessed 23 December 2019] What does mindfulness meditation do to your brain? Scientific American Blog Network

[Online] https://blogs.scientificamerican.com/guest-blog/what-does-mindfulness-meditation-do-to-your-brain/ (archived at https://perma.cc/CUL8-Z26H)

Longe, O *et al* (2010) Having a word with yourself: Neural correlates of self-criticism and self-reassurance, *NeuroImage*, 49 (2), pp 1849–56

MacKian, S (2002) [accessed 4 February 2020] A review of health seeking behaviour: Problems and prospects [Online] https://assets.publishing.service.gov.uk/media/57a08d1de5274a27b200163d/05-03_health_seeking_behaviour.pdf (archived at https://perma.cc/HN8N-TWWA)

McGuire, JB and Tang, V (2011) [accessed 4 January 2020] Slow down to speed up, *Forbes* [Online] www.forbes.com/2011/02/23/slow-down-speed-efficiency-leadership-managing-ccl.html#5ddec8ea4be1 (archived at https://perma.cc/7656-H7S9)

Newport, C (2016) *Deep Work: Rules for focused success in a distracted world*, Piaktus, London

Paul, K (2019) [accessed 4 February 2020] Microsoft Japan tested a four-day work week and productivity jumped by 40%, *The Guardian* [Online] www.theguardian.com/technology/2019/nov/04/microsoft-japan-four-day-work-week-productivity (archived at https://perma.cc/DS6L-UNHA)

Singh, J, Goolsby, JR and Rhoads, GK (1994) Behavioral and psychological consequences of boundary spanning burnout for customer service representatives, *Journal of Marketing Research*, 31 (4), pp 558–69

Swart, T, Chisholm, K and Brown, P (2015) *Neuroscience for Leadership: Harnessing the brain gain advantage*, Palgrave, Basingstoke

Tolle, E (2019) *The Power of Now: A guide to spiritual enlightenment*, New World Library, San Francisco

Zomerland, G (2014) [accessed 6 February 2020] H.A.L.T. (Hungry, Angry, Lonely and Tired): A self-care tool, *Healthy Psych* [Online] https://healthypsych.com/h-a-l-t-hungry-angry-lonely-and-tired-a-self-care-tool/ (archived at https://perma.cc/R5D8-S9TP)

Chapter Six

Berger, PL and Luckmann, T (1966) *The Social Construction of Reality: A treatise in the sociology of knowledge*, Doubleday & Company, New York

Bonchek, M (2016) [accessed 3 January 2020] Why the problem with learning is unlearning, *Harvard Business Review* [Online] https://hbr.org/2016/11/why-the-problem-with-learning-is-unlearning (archived at https://perma.cc/LU8D-PAJH)

Bono, G, Emmons, RA and McCullough, ME (2012) Gratitude in practice and the practice of gratitude, in *Positive Psychology in Practice*, ed PA Linley and S Joseph, pp 464–81, John Wiley & Sons, Hoboken, NJ

Boyd, R and Myers, J (1988) Transformative education, *International Journal of Lifelong Education*, 7 (4), pp 261–84

Brewer, JA *et al* (2011) Mindfulness training for smoking cessation: Results from a randomized controlled trial, *Drug and Alcohol Dependence*, **119** (1–2), pp 72–80

Clem, RL and Schiller, D (2016) New learning and unlearning: Strangers or accomplices in threat memory attenuation? *Trends in Neurosciences*, **39** (5), pp 340–51

Druckman, D and Bjork, RA (1994) *Learning, Remembering, Believing: Enhanced human performance*, National Academies Press, Washington, DC

Flower, J (1999) [accessed 3 February 2020] In the mush, *Physician Executive*, **25** (1), p 64 [Online] http://connection.ebscohost.com/c/articles/1560025 (archived at https://perma.cc/G8C9-2Q87)

Goleman, D (1996) *Emotional Intelligence: Why it can matter more than IQ*, Bloomsbury Publishing, London

Harris, S (2014) *Waking Up: A guide to spirituality without religion*, Simon and Schuster, New York

Hofmann, SG, Grossman, P and Hinton, DE (2011) Loving-kindness and compassion meditation: Potential for psychological interventions, *Clinical Psychology Review*, **31** (7), pp 1126–32

Irvine, WB (2009) *A Guide to the Good Life: The ancient art of stoic joy*, Oxford University Press, Oxford

Kross, E *et al* (2014) Self-talk as a regulatory mechanism: How you do it matters, *Journal of Personality and Social Psychology*, **106** (2), pp 304 –24

Leaviss, J and Uttley, L (2015) Psychotherapeutic benefits of compassion-focused therapy: An early systematic review, *Psychological Medicine*, **45** (5), pp 927–945

Little, W (2012) [accessed 3 January 2020] Society and social interaction, in *Introduction to Sociology*, ed W Little, chapter 4, OpenStax College,

open source [Online] https://opentextbc.ca/introductiontosociology/
chapter/chapter4-society-and-social-interaction/#section4.3 (archived
at https://perma.cc/6GT6-C9H9)

Martin-Cuellar, A (2018) [accessed 14 April 2020] Self-reflexivity through
journaling: An imperative process for the practicing clinician, *The
William & Mary Educational Review*, 5 (1), article 11 [Online] https://
pdfs.semanticscholar.org/826c/cad19d601af4f4747a6c7dd527cc
4958cd73.pdf (archived at https://perma.cc/QY8Z-S5F7)

Moran, BP and Lennington, M (2013) *The 12 Week Year: Get more done
in 12 weeks than others do in 12 months*, Wiley, Hoboken, NJ

Newstrom, J (1983) The management of unlearning: Exploding the 'clean
slate' fallacy, *Training and Development Journal*, 37 (8), pp 36–39

Noetel, M *et al* (2019) Mindfulness and acceptance approaches to
sporting performance enhancement: A systematic review, *International
Review of Sport and Exercise Psychology*, 12 (1), pp 139–75

Oh, B *et al* (2017) Health and well-being benefits of spending time in
forests: Systematic review, *Environmental Health and Preventive
Medicine*, 22, article 71, doi: 10.1186/s12199-017-0677-9

Reio, TG and Wiswell, A (2000) Field investigation of the relationship
among adult curiosity, workplace learning, and job performance,
Human Resource Development Quarterly, 11 (1), pp 5–30

Smernoff, E *et al* (2015) The effects of 'the work' meditation (Byron
Katie) on psychological symptoms and quality of life: A pilot clinical
study, *Explore: The Journal of Science and Healing*, 11 (1), pp 24–31

Suzuki, S *et al* (1970) *Zen Mind, Beginner's Mind*, Weatherhill, Fairfield,
CT

Uvnäs-Moberg, K, Handlin, L and Petersson, M (2014) [accessed 14 April
2020] Self-soothing behaviors with particular reference to oxytocin
release induced by non-noxious sensory stimulation, *Frontiers in
Psychology* [Online] doi: 10.3389/fpsyg.2014.01529

Chapter Seven

Barton, D, Grant, A and Horn, M (2012) [accessed 5 January 2020]
Leading in the 21st century, *McKinsey Quarterly* [Online] www.
mckinsey.com/featured-insights/leadership/leading-in-the-21st-century
(archived at https://perma.cc/8ATR-ADKQ)

Chowdhury, MR (2020) [accessed 5 January 2020] What is mental contrasting and how to benefit from it? [Online] https://positive psychology.com/mental-contrasting/ (archived at https://perma. cc/746W-7VQ3)

Cialdini, RB (2006) *Influence: The psychology of persuasion*, Harper Collins, New York

Cross, A and Sheffield, D (2019) Mental contrasting for health behaviour change: A systematic review and meta-analysis of effects and moderator variables, *Health Psychology Review*, **13** (2), pp 209–25

García, H (2017) *Ikigai: The Japanese secret to a long and happy life*, Hutchinson, London

Graham, P (2009) [accessed 5 January 2020] Maker's schedule, manager's schedule [Online] www.paulgraham.com/makersschedule.html (archived at https://perma.cc/9RP6-MVPL)

Hendricks, G (2009) *The Big Leap: Conquer your hidden fear and take life to the next level*, HarperOne, San Francisco

Kashtan, I and Kashtan, M (nd) [accessed 29 December 2019] Key assumptions and intentions of NVC [Online] https://baynvc.org/ key-assumptions-and-intentions-of-nvc/ (archived at https://perma.cc/ YWJ4-T6RT)

Litvin, R (nd) [accessed 5 January 2020] Energy audit [Online] https:// richlitvin.com/wp-content/uploads/2018/08/Energy-Audit-Tool-bw.pdf (archived at https://perma.cc/6Q46-H69P)

Morphew, CC and Hartley, M (2006) Mission statements: A thematic analysis of rhetoric across institutional type, *The Journal of Higher Education*, **77** (3), pp 456–71

Oettingen, G (2014) *Rethinking Positive Thinking: Inside the new science of motivation*, Penguin, New York

Oettingen, G and Reininger, KM (2016) The power of prospection: Mental contrasting and behavior change, *Social and Personality Psychology Compass*, **10** (11), pp 591–604

Perlow, LA, Noonan Hadley, C and Eun, E (2017) [accessed 5 January 2020] Stop the meeting madness, *Harvard Business Review* [Online] https://hbr.org/2017/07/stop-the-meeting-madness (archived at https:// perma.cc/7J7A-5F52)

Peterson, DB (2010) Reflection Calendar: Good to great coaching – Accelerating the journey, in *Advancing Executive Coaching: Setting the course for successful leadership coaching*, ed G Hernez-Broome and LA Boyce, pp 83–102, Jossey-Bass, San Francisco

Rosenberg, M (2015) *Nonviolent Communication: A language of life – Life-changing tools for healthy relationships*, PuddleDancer Press, Encinitas, CA

Vohs, KD *et al* (2017) Problems with positive thinking and how to overcome them: The role of self-regulation in financial well-being, in *Handbook of Self-Regulation*, 3rd edn: *Research, Theory, and Applications*, ed KD Vohs and RF Baumeister, pp 547–70, Guilford Publications, New York

Wiest, B (2018) [accessed 7 February 2020] How to get into the 'zone of genius' and unlock your highest potential, *Forbes* [Online] www. forbes.com/sites/briannawiest/2018/09/26/how-to-get-into-the-zone-of-genius-and-unlock-your-highest-potential/#7b2068d65672 (archived at https://perma.cc/2V6P-XHW7)

Chapter Eight

Askvik, S (2002) [accessed 4 February 2020] The Success Trap in organizational learning: cognitive and political explanations [Online] https://warwick.ac.uk/fac/soc/wbs/conf/olkc/archive/oklc3/papers/id222.pdf (archived at https://perma.cc/DN49-SLBQ)

Barton, D, Grant, A and Horn, M (2012) [accessed 5 January 2020] Leading in the 21st century, *McKinsey Quarterly* [Online] www. mckinsey.com/featured-insights/leadership/leading-in-the-21st-century (archived at https://perma.cc/8ATR-ADKQ)

Bennett, N and Lemoine, GJ (2014) [accessed 11 January 2020] What VUCA really means for you, *Harvard Business Review* [Online] https://hbr.org/2014/01/what-vuca-really-means-for-you (archived at https://perma.cc/DL68-QXAJ)

Bochner, S (1965) Defining intolerance of ambiguity, *Psychological Record*, **15** (3), pp 393–400

Brown, P (2014) [accessed 4 February 2020] Why entrepreneurs are the most risk-averse people, *Inc* [Online] www.inc.com/paul-brown/entrepreneurs-most-risk-averse-people-on-the-planet.html (archived at https://perma.cc/U3K6-KR6B)

Clifford, C (2019) [accessed 10 February 2020] Elon Musk on SpaceX: 'I always thought we would fail', *CNBC* [Online] www.cnbc.com/2019/03/06/elon-musk-on-spacex-i-always-thought-we-would-fail.html (archived at https://perma.cc/R776-PWVX)

Dowling, JM and Yap, CF (2012) *Happiness and Poverty in Developing Countries: A global perspective*, Palgrave Macmillan, Basingstoke

Fenton, R and Waltz, A (2010) *Go for No! Yes is the destination, no is how you get there*, Courage Crafters Inc., Orlando, FL

Kahneman, D, Knetsch, JL and Thaler, RH (1991) The endowment effect, loss aversion, and status quo bias, *Journal of Economic Perspectives*, 5 (1), pp 193–206

Kierkegaard, S (1844) *The Concept of Anxiety: A simple psychologically oriented deliberation in view of the dogmatic problem of hereditary sin*, no publisher details

Richards, C (2013) [accessed 4 February 2020] Overcoming an aversion to loss, *New York Times* [Online] www.nytimes.com/2013/12/09/your-money/overcoming-an-aversion-to-loss.html (archived at https://perma.cc/4JW7-MJCN)

Sarasvathy, S (2014) [accessed 10 January 2020] Entrepreneurship: (Not) risky business (video), Darden School of Business (University of Virginia) [Online] www.youtube.com/watch?v=3IJlHfw43mQ (archived at https://perma.cc/D9RG-EV2K)

Sen, A (2001) *Development as Freedom*, Oxford University Press, Oxford

Shedd, JA (1928) *Salt from My Attic*, The Mosher Press, Portland, MA

Sinek, S (2019) *The Infinite Game*, Penguin Random House, New York

Tversky, A and Kahneman, D (1991) Loss aversion in riskless choice: A reference-dependent model, *The Quarterly Journal of Economics*, **106** (4), pp 1039–61

Xu, H and Tracey, TJG (2015) Career decision ambiguity tolerance scale: Construction and initial validations, *Journal of Vocational Behavior*, 88, pp 1–9

Chapter Nine

Cacciotti, G and Hayton, JC (2015) Fear and entrepreneurship: A review and research agenda, *International Journal of Management Reviews*, 17 (2), pp 165–90

De Mol, E, Ho, VT and Pollack, JM (2018) Predicting entrepreneurial burnout in a moderated mediated model of job fit, *Journal of Small Business Management*, **56** (3), pp 392–411

Erikson, T (2002) Entrepreneurial capital: The emerging venture's most important asset and competitive advantage, *Journal of Business Venturing*, **17** (3), pp 275–90

Hendricks, G (2009) *The Big Leap: Conquer your hidden fear and take life to the next level*, Harper One, San Francisco

Jarvis, P (2019) *Company of One: Why staying small is the next big thing for business*, Penguin, London

Kerr, SP, Kerr, WR and Xu, T (2017) [accessed 14 April 2020] Personality traits of entrepreneurs: A review of recent literature, NBER Working Paper no. 24097 [Online] www.nber.org/papers/w24097 (archived at https://perma.cc/ZSG6-ML4U)

Koulopoulos, T (2015) [accessed 12 January 2020] Up next: The greatest era of entrepreneurship and small business the world has ever seen, *Inc* [Online] www.inc.com/thomas-koulopoulos/up-next-the-greatest-era-of-entrepreneurship-and-small-business-the-world-has-ev.html (archived at https://perma.cc/N6MP-M4HB)

Mansfield, M (2019) [accessed 12 January 2020] Startup statistics: The numbers you need to know, *Small Business Trends* [Online] https://smallbiztrends.com/2019/03/startup-statistics-small-business.html (archived at https://perma.cc/NJ7R-YR9L)

Priestley, D (2013) *Entrepreneur Revolution: How to develop your entrepreneurial mindset and start a business that works*, Capstone Publishing, Chichester

Read, S *et al* (2016) *Effectual Entrepreneurship*, Routledge, Oxford

Schumpeter, J (1942) *Capitalism, Socialism, and Democracy*, Harper & Bros, New York

Shirey, MR (2009) Transferable skills and entrepreneurial strategy, *Clinical Nurse Specialist*, **23** (3), pp 128–30

Suárez-Álvarez, J and Pedrosa, I (2016) The assessment of entrepreneurial personality: The current situation and future directions, **37** (1), pp 62–68

Von Stumm, S (2018) Better open than intellectual: The benefits of investment personality traits for learning, *Personality & Social Psychology Bulletin*, **44** (4), pp 562–73

Xu, H and Tracey, TJG (2015) Career decision ambiguity tolerance scale: Construction and initial validations, *Journal of Vocational Behavior*, 88, pp 1–9

Chapter Ten

Barton, D, Grant, A and Horn, M (2012) [accessed 5 January 2020] Leading in the 21st century, *McKinsey Quarterly* [Online] www. mckinsey.com/featured-insights/leadership/leading-in-the-21st-century (archived at https://perma.cc/8ATR-ADKQ)

Bowlby, J (1988) *A Secure Base: Clinical applications of attachment theory*, Routledge, Oxford

Carse, JP (2012) *Finite and Infinite Games: A vision of life as play and possibility*, Free Press, New York

De Haan, E (2014) *Leadership Shadow: How to recognise and avoid derailment, hubris and overdrive*, Kogan Page, London

Delach Leonard, M (2014) [accessed 15 January 2020] How a Clayton manufacturer shared sacrifice to avoid layoffs during the Great Recession, *St Louis Public Radio* [Online] https://news.stlpublicradio.org/post/how-clayton-manufacturer-shared-sacrifice-avoid-layoffs-during-great-recession#stream/0 (archived at https://perma.cc/3HR3-M2AG)

Edmondson, A (2018a) [accessed 15 January 2020] The importance of psychological safety, *HR Magazine* [Online] www.hrmagazine.co.uk/article-details/the-importance-of-psychological-safety (archived at https://perma.cc/A9LN-SGUG)

Edmondson, A (2018b) *The Fearless Organization: Creating psychological safety in the workplace for learning, innovation, and growth*, John Wiley & Sons, New York

Eluard, P (2005) *Les yeux fertiles: Suite*, Cercle d'art, Paris

Etzioni, A (2011) Behavioural economics: Next steps, *Journal of Consumer Policy*, 34, pp 277–87

Herbert, W (2008) Arranging for serenity: How physical space and emotion intersect, *Scientific American Mind*, 19 (4), pp 80–81

Herway, J (2019) [accessed 17 January 2020] How to create a culture of psychological safety, *Gallup Workplace* [Online] www.gallup.com/workplace/236198/create-culture-psychological-safety.aspx (archived at https://perma.cc/57H4-F94E)

IBM (2010) [accessed 4 January 2020] Capitalizing on Complexity: Insights from the Global Chief Executive Officer Study [Online] www.ibm.com/downloads/cas/1VZV5X8J (archived at https://perma.cc/K4TF-6ANL)

Mitchell, P (2011) *The 10 Laws of Career Reinvention: Essential survival skills for any economy*, Prentice Hall Press, Upper Saddle River, NJ

Nickerson, RS (1998) Confirmation bias: A ubiquitous phenomenon in many guises, *Review of General Psychology*, 2 (2), pp 175–220

Origin and meaning of productivity (nd) [accessed 4 February 2020] *Online Etymology Dictionary* [Online] www.etymonline.com/word/productivity (archived at https://perma.cc/R6ZY-G45E)

Rantanen, J et al (2011) Introducing theoretical approaches to work-life balance and testing a new typology among professionals, in *Creating Balance? International Perspectives on the Work-Life Integration of Professionals*, ed S Kaiser, M Ringlstetter, D Eikhof and M Pina e Cunha, pp 27–46, Springer Heidelberg, Berlin

Rozovsky, J (2015) [accessed 5 February 2020] The five keys to a successful Google team, *re:work* [Online] https://rework.withgoogle.com/blog/five-keys-to-a-successful-google-team/ (archived at https://perma.cc/4KPS-25AP)

Sherman, S and Freas, A (2004) [accessed 15 January 2020] The Wild West of executive coaching, *Harvard Business Review* [Online] https://hbr.org/2004/11/the-wild-west-of-executive-coaching (archived at https://perma.cc/PAU6-SG8L)

Sinek, S (2014) [accessed 17 January 2020] Why good leaders make you feel safe, *TED Talk* [Online] www.ted.com/talks/simon_sinek_why_good_leaders_make_you_feel_safe/transcript?language=en (archived at https://perma.cc/SL5D-WBMH)

Sinek, S (2019) *The Infinite Game*, Penguin Random House, New York

Sturrock, J (2018) [accessed 15 January 2020] Cultural issues related to allegations of bullying and harassment in NHS Highland: Independent review report [Online] www.gov.scot/publications/report-cultural-issues-related-allegations-bullying-harassment-nhs-highland/pages/45/ (archived at https://perma.cc/64C3-JUGW)

Van Rompay, TJL and Jol, T (2016) Wild and free: Unpredictability and spaciousness as predictors of creative performance, *Journal of Environmental Psychology*, 48, pp 140–48

Whyte, D (1994) *The Heart Aroused: Poetry and the preservation of the soul in corporate America*, Currency Doubleday, New York

Whyte, D (2009) *The Three Marriages: Reimagining work, self and relationship*, Riverhead Books, Hull

Zantal-Wiener, A (2017) [accessed 17 January 2020] A brief history of productivity: How getting stuff done became an industry, *Hubspot* [Online] https://blog.hubspot.com/marketing/a-brief-history-of-productivity (archived at https://perma.cc/U6A3-2C7E)

Zetlin, M (2020) [accessed 17 Janaury 2020] Got a to-do list? Great! A not-to-do list is even more important, *Inc* [Online] www.inc.com/minda-zetlin/got-a-to-do-list-great-a-not-to-do-list-is-even-more-important.html (archived at https://perma.cc/FZT9-G4C9)

INDEX